"And with that wonderful audacity of youth, I went to Hollywood, arriving there with just forty dollars. It was a big day the day I got on that Santa Fe California Limited. I was just free and happy!"

—Walt Disney, on embarking for California in 1923 to fulfill his dreams

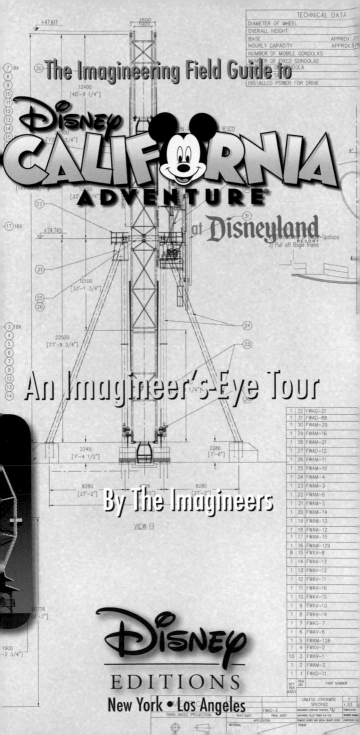

The Imagineering Field Guide to

DISNEY CALIFORNIA ADVENTURE

at Disneyland RESORT

An Imagineer's-Eye Tour

By The Imagineers

DISNEP
EDITIONS

New York • Los Angeles

TECHNICAL DATA

DIAMETER OF WHEEL
OVERALL HEIGHT
BASE   APPROX 2
HOURLY CAPACITY   APPROX 97
NUMBER OF MOBILE GONDOLAS
NUMBER OF FIXED GONDOLAS
              GONDOLA
INSTALLED POWER FOR DRIVE

For information address Disney Editions,
1101 Flower Street, Glendale, California 91201.

Editorial Director: Wendy Lefkon
Editor: Jessica Ward

Written and designed by Alex Wright with help from all the Imagineers
For everybody who's ever played a part in helping me pursue my dreams

The author would like to thank Jason Surrell for his ongoing support; Scott Otis for the continued use of his extensive Disney library; Jody Revenson for giving him a start in this business; Wendy Lefkon and Jessica Ward for all of their work behind the scenes; David Buckley for the use of his Sorcerer Mickey illustration on the cover; Denise Brown for always being there to answer an image question; Marty Sklar, Tom Fitzgerald, and Bruce Vaughn for their input and for letting him do another one of these; Dave Fisher, Sarah Farmer Earll, and Frank Reifsnyder for their thorough review; Dave Durham, John Dennis, Matt Meyer, Robert Shmerling, David Taylor, Paul Beasley, Scott Mallwitz, Michael Crawford, David Stofcik, Jose Morales, John Higgins, and Ken Petersen for answering random questions out of the blue; Kim, Finn, and Lincoln for giving Daddy the time to work on his book; and all Imagineers past and present for their assistance and for all the inspiration they've provided through the years.

ISBN 978–1–4231–8000–5
H106-9333-5-14017
Printed in Malaysia
First Edition
10 9 8 7 6 5 4 3 2 1

Visit www.disneybooks.com

TABLE OF CONTENTS

IMAGINEERING 101 — 6
THE HISTORY, LANGUAGE, AND UNIQUE CULTURE OF WALT'S DREAM FACTORY

DISNEY CALIFORNIA ADVENTURE — 14
THE AMAZING STORIES OF AN AMAZING PLACE WHERE DISNEY'S DREAMS CAME TRUE

BUENA VISTA STREET — 24
SEE CALIFORNIA THE WAY WALT MIGHT HAVE SEEN IT IN 1923

CONDOR FLATS — 34
THE EXCITEMENT OF NEW FRONTIERS IN AVIATION

GRIZZLY PEAK — 42
EXPERIENCE THE INVIGORATING GREAT OUTDOORS OF THIS GREAT STATE

PARADISE PIER — 52
A CLASSIC SEASIDE AMUSEMENT PIER WITH A DISNEY SPIN, AND LOOP, AND DROP…

PACIFIC WHARF — 76
A TASTE OF THE NORTHERN CALIFORNIA COAST

CARS LAND — 86
HANG OUT WITH YOUR FOUR-WHEELED FRIENDS IN RADIATOR SPRINGS

"A BUG'S LAND" — 98
GET A BUG'S-EYE VIEW OF THE WORLD WITH FLIK AND THE GANG

HOLLYWOOD LAND — 110
EXPLORE CALIFORNIA'S VERY OWN DREAM FACTORY

BIBLIOGRAPHY — 128

WDI Disciplines

Imagineers form a diverse organization, with over 140 different job titles working toward the common goal of telling great stories and creating great places. WDI has a broad collection of disciplines considering its size, due to the highly specialized nature of our work. In everything it does, WDI is supported by many other divisions of The Walt Disney Company.

Early Cars Land sketch by Chris Turner

Show/Concept Design and Illustration produces the early drawings and renderings that serve as the inspiration for our projects, and provides the initial concepts and visual communication. This artwork gives the entire team a shared vision.

Show Writing develops the stories we want to tell in the Parks, as well as any nomenclature that is required. This group writes the scripts for our attractions, the copy for plaques, and names our lands, rides, shops, vehicles, and restaurants.

Architecture turns all of those fanciful show drawings into real buildings, meeting all of the functional requirements that are expected of them. Our Parks and resorts present some unique architectural challenges.

Carthay Circle Theatre elevation

Interior concept for Carthay Circle Restaurant

Interior Designers are responsible for the design details on the inside of our buildings. They develop the look and feel of interior spaces, and select finishes, furniture, and fixtures to complete the design.

Engineering disciplines at WDI set our mechanical, electrical, and other standards and make all of our ideas work. Engineers design structures and systems for our buildings, bridges, ride systems, and play spaces, and solve the tricky problems we throw their way every day.

Support trusses of California Screamin'

Lighting Design puts all the hard work the rest of us have done on our shows and attractions into the best light. Lighting designers are also responsible for specifying all of the themed lighting fixtures found in the Parks. As our lighting designers are fond of telling us, "Without lights, it's radio!"

Cars Land at night

Sign over Buena Vista Street

Graphic Designers produce signage, both flat and dimensional, in addition to providing lots of the artwork, patterns, and details that finish the Disney show. Marquees and directional signs are just a couple of examples of their work.

Prop Design is concerned with who "lives" in a given area of a Park or resort. All of the pieces and parts of everyday life that tell you about a person, a time, or a place are very carefully selected and placed. These props have to be found, purchased, prepped, built, and installed.

Workshop shelves in Fly 'n' Buy

Sound is a huge part of the fun at Mater's Junkyard Jamboree.

Sound Designers work to develop the auditory backdrop for everything you see and experience. The songs in the attractions, the background music in each of the lands, and the sound effects built into show elements all work together to complete our illusions. Sound is one of the most evocative senses.

Media Design creates for us all of the various film, video, audio, and on-screen interactive content in our Parks. WDI features its own in-house production studio to fill those needs on our projects.

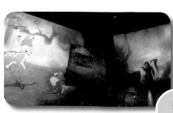

Preshow at Disney Animation

9

Landscape Architecture is the discipline that focuses on our tree and plant palette and area development. This includes the layout of all of our hardscape as well as the arrangement of the foliage elements in our lands and attractions.

Show Set Design takes concepts and breaks them down into bite-size pieces that are organized into drawing and drafting packages; integrated into the architectural, mechanical, civil, or other components of the project; and tracked during fabrication.

Hyperion Bridge design details

Character Paint creates the reproductions of various materials, finishes, and states of aging whenever we need to make something new look old.

Character Plaster produces the hard finishes in the Park that mimic other materials. This includes rockwork, themed paving, and architectural facades such as faux stone and plaster. They even use concrete to imitate wood!

Dimensional Design is the art of model-making and sculpture. This skill is used to work out design issues ahead of time in model form, ensuring that our relative scales and spatial relationships are properly coordinated. Models are a wonderful tool for problem-solving.

Radiator Springs and Ornament Valley model for Cars Land

Fabrication Design involves developing and implementing the production strategies that allow us to build all the specialized items on the large and complex projects that we deliver. Somebody has to figure out how to build the impossible!

Special Effects creates all of the magical (but totally believable) smoke, fire, water, lightning, ghosts, explosions, pixie dust, wind, rainfall, snow, and other mechanical tricks that give our stories action and a sense of surprise. Some of these effects are quite simple, while others rely on the most sophisticated technologies drawn from the field of entertainment or any other imaginable industry.

Waterfall in Grizzly Peak

Production drawing by Mike Sheehan

Production Design starts with the show design, takes it to the next level of detail, and ensures that it can be built so as to maintain the creative intent. It also has the task of integrating the show with all the other systems that will need to be coordinated in the field during installation.

Master Planning looks into the future and maps out the best locations and layouts for a Park or a whole property. In fact, they see further into the future than any other Imagineering division, often planning locations for projects that might be many years away from realization.

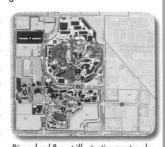

Disneyland Resort illustrative master plan

R&D stands for Research & Development. WDI R&D, Inc. is a sister company to WDI that gets to play with the coolest toys. They investigate all the latest technologies from every field of study and look for ways to apply them to Disney entertainment, often inventing new ways to utilize those developments. R&D serves as a resource for the entire Company.

Project Management is responsible for organizing our teams, schedules, and processes so that our projects can be delivered when they're supposed to be, within a financial framework, on schedule, and at the expected level of quality.

Construction Management ensures that every job meets Disney construction standards, including quality control, code compliance, and long-term durability during operation.

Imagineering Lingo

WDI has a very vibrant and unique culture, which is even embodied in the terms we throw around the office when we're working. Here is a guide to help you understand us a bit better as we show you around the Park.

Area Development - The interstitial spaces between the attractions, restaurants, and shops. This includes landscape architecture, propping, show elements, and special enhancements intended to expand the experience.

Audio-Animatronics® Figures - The term for the three-dimensional animated human and animal characters we employ to perform in our shows and attractions. Audio-Animatronics technology was invented by Imagineers at Walt's request and is an essential component of many iconic Disney attractions.

Berm - A raised earthen barrier, typically heavily landscaped, which serves to eliminate visual intrusions into the Park from the outside world and block the outside world from intruding inside.

BGM - Background Music. The musical selections that fill in the audio landscape as you make your way around the Park. Each BGM track is carefully selected, arranged, and recorded to enhance the story being told, or the area you have entered.

Blue Sky - The early stages in the idea-generation process when anything is possible. There are not yet any considerations taken into account that might rein in the creative process. At this point, the sky's the limit!

Brainstorm - A gathering for the purpose of generating as many ideas as possible in the shortest time possible. We hold many brainstorming sessions at WDI, always looking for the best ideas. Imagineering has a set of Brainstorming Rules, which are always adhered to.

> **Rule 1 -** There is no such thing as a bad idea. We never know how one idea (however far-fetched) might lead into another one that is exactly right.
> **Rule 2 -** We don't talk yet about *why not*. There will be plenty of time for realities later, so we don't want them to get in the way of the good ideas now.
> **Rule 3 -** Nothing should stifle the flow of ideas. No buts or can'ts or other "stopping" words. We want to hear words such as "and," "or," and "what if?"
> **Rule 4 -** There is no such thing as a bad idea. (We take that one very seriously.)

Charrette - Another term for a brainstorming session. From the French word for "cart." It refers to the cart sent through the Latin Quarter in Paris to collect the art and design projects of students at the legendary École des Beaux-Arts who were unable to deliver them to the school themselves after the mad rush to complete their work at the end of the term.

Concept - An idea and the effort put into communicating it and developing it into something usable. A concept can be expressed as a drawing, a written description, or simply a verbal pitch. Everything we do starts out as a concept.

Dark Ride - A term often used to describe the charming Fantasyland attractions, among others, housed more or less completely inside a show building, which allows for greater isolation of show elements and light control, as needed.

> **E-Ticket** - The top level of attractions. This dates back to an early Disneyland ticketing system used to distribute ridership through all attractions in the Park. Each was assigned a letter (A,B,C,D,E) indicating where it fell in the Park's pecking order.

> **Elevation** - A drawing of a true frontal view of an object—usually a building—often drawn from multiple sides, eliminating the perspective that you would see in the real world, for clarity in the design and to lead construction activities.

Kinetics - Movement and motion in a scene that give it life and energy. This can come from moving vehicles, active signage, changes in the lighting, special effects, or even hanging banners or flags that move around as the wind blows.

Maquette - A model, especially a sculpture, depicting a show element in miniature scale so that design issues can be worked out before construction begins. It's much easier to make changes on a maquette than on a full-size anything.

Plan - A direct overhead view of an object or a space. Very useful in verifying relative sizes of elements and the flow of guests and show elements through an area.

Plussing - A word derived from Walt's penchant for always trying to make an idea better. Imagineers are continually trying to *plus* their work, even after it's "finished."

POV - Point Of View. The position from which something is seen, or the place an artist chooses to use as the vantage point of the imaginary viewer in a concept illustration. POVs are chosen in order to best represent the idea being shown.

Propping - The placement of objects around a scene. From books on a shelf to place settings on a table to wall hangings in an office space, props are the elements that give a set life and describe the people who live there. They are the everyday objects we see all around but that point out so much about our story if you pay attention to them.

Section - A drawing that looks as if it's a slice through an object or space. This is very helpful in seeing how various elements interrelate. It is typically drawn as though it were an elevation, with heavier line weights defining where our imaginary cut would be.

Show - Everything we put "onstage" in a Disney Park. Walt believed that everything we put out for the guests in our Parks was part of a big show, so much of our terminology originated in the show business world. With that in mind, *show* becomes for us a very broad term that includes just about anything our guests see, hear, smell, or come in contact with during their visit to any of our Parks or resorts.

Story - Story is the fundamental building block of everything WDI does. Imagineers are, above all, storytellers. The time, place, characters, and plot points that give our work meaning start with the story, which is also the framework that guides all design decisions.

Storyboard - A large pinup board used to post ideas in a charrette or to outline the story points of a ride or film. The technique was perfected by Walt in the early days of his animation Studio and became a staple of the animated film development process. The practice naturally transferred over to WDI when so many of the early Imagineers came over from Walt's Animation department.

Theme - The fundamental nature of a story in terms of what it means to us, or the choice of time, place, and decor applied to an area in order to support that story.

THRC - Theoretical Hourly Ride Capacity. The number of guests per hour that can experience an attraction under optimal conditions. THRC is always taken into account when a new attraction is under consideration.

Visual Intrusion - Any outside element that makes its way into a scene, breaks the visual continuity, and destroys the illusion. WDI works hard to eliminate visual intrusions.

Wienie - Walt's playful term for a visual element that could be used to draw people into and around a space. A wienie is big enough to be seen from a distance and interesting enough to make you want to take a closer look, like the Carthay Circle Theatre at the end of Buena Vista Street. Wienies are critical to our efforts at laying out a sequence of experiences in an organized fashion.

DISNEY CALIFORNIA ADVENTURE

Disney California Adventure pays homage to the amazing state in which it is found. It's a place that holds a great deal of meaning for all of the Disney Parks because it held great meaning for Walt Disney himself as he set off to pursue his dreams. This is where he honed his craft of storytelling with the entire world as his audience.

Main entrance concept by Ray Spencer

California Dreaming and Doing

The state of California holds a unique place in the conscience of the United States and even the world. It is the third largest geographically and most populous of the fifty states in this country. It carries considerable economic weight, accounting for roughly 13% of the U.S. gross domestic product—with a total that would rank it in the top 10% in the world if it were a country unto itself. And in terms of pop culture, California has always been on the leading edge due to the high concentration of media industries, most notably the massive "Hollywood" motion picture business that has been inextricably linked to the identity of California since its founding during the early years of the twentieth century.

It is also the real home of The Walt Disney Company, which was founded in Los Angeles in 1923 by Walt Disney and his brother, Roy O. Disney. Though today the Company is truly global, with operations and distribution of its many products and offerings in just about every part of the world, its base remains where Walt established it all those years ago. The connection to the rest of the entertainment industry, the proximity of Disneyland, and the longstanding ties between the Company and the community ensure that this will remain the Company's home for years to come. This is why California is such a fitting subject for a Disney Park!

The Park also fulfills an important role as the neighbor and counterpart to Disneyland Park, located across the Esplanade from its front gates. This is no small task. Disneyland, since its opening in 1955, has been an iconic landmark in the popular culture worldwide. Imagineering's original foray into environmental experiences, it ushered in a new form of family entertainment that has been synonymous with the Company itself. Disneyland is unique in all the world, so the bar is set very high for any Park that takes up residence next door.

Through Rose-Tinted Sunglasses

So, in 2001, Walt Disney Imagineering debuted Disney California Adventure, dedicating it to all of these ideals embodied by the state of California and to our Company's relationship to it. From the beginning Disney California Adventure has captured the energy and the excitement of the Golden State, and ongoing work has strengthened the Park's connection to the Company's history. The Park carries on these ideas through the presentation of an optimistic series of expressions of the variety of experiences and textures that can be found in California. It tells stories about the varied places, the diverse people, and the rich history of this amazing state. As with most of our work, it presents an idealized vision of the times and of the places that each portion of the Park represents.

This form of heightened reality is a hallmark of the Disney Park experience. It began with the depiction of Main Street, U.S.A. as a *better* version of the Marceline, Missouri, of Walt's youth. These venues offer entertainment with a point of view that makes one believe that tomorrow will be a better day—so we can believe that California's future will be just as remarkable as its past.

QUICK TAKES

- Disney California Adventure opened on February 8, 2001. It was the eighth Disney Park in the world.

- The original name of "Disney's California Adventure" was updated to "Disney California Adventure" in May of 2010.

- Disney California Adventure covers roughly fifty-five acres of land.

Bird's-eye of the reimagined Disney California Adventure by Anastasia Pavlova

Walt and Roy Disney in front of their Kingswell Avenue studio

Golden State of Mind

The Walt Disney Company has longstanding connections to the state of California. From the time Walt stepped off that train in 1923 right up to today, the Company has maintained a significant presence in Southern California. Disney facilities and venues can be found throughout the region, and the man and the Company have left an indelible mark on the entertainment industry, on popular culture, and on other institutions. Other Disney venues have come and gone, but remain part of the history of this place. Some of those connections between the Company and the Los Angeles area are referenced in the Park itself, and together they all tell a story of a fantastic journey.

In the summer of 1923, Walt made the big move from Kansas City to California. Initially, he lived in a room at his Uncle Robert's house in a bungalow on Kingswell Avenue in Silver Lake. He spent time experimenting with a camera in the garage and backyard of that home. When he convinced his brother Roy to join him in his business ventures, the two of them set up the first Disney Brothers Studio, in a rented space also on Kingswell, just up the street from Uncle Robert's.

Following their first successes with the Oswald cartoons, in 1926 Walt and Roy purchased nearly identical mirror-image homes side-by-side on Lyric Avenue in Los Feliz, just around the corner from the site on Hyperion Avenue where they had begun to build the Studio that would house their operations from 1926 to 1940. Walt would live in the house on Lyric until 1933, when he and his wife, Lillian, moved to a much grander Tudor-styled home on Woking Way in the hills above Loz Feliz, still very near the Studio site. From there, Walt moved to a home on Carolwood Drive. It was here that he built the famed backyard railway that was one of the components of his evolving visions for an entertainment complex that became Disneyland.

Branching Out

The year 1940 saw the big move to the current site of the Walt Disney Studios in Burbank. This large lot and the initial build out were financed largely through the profits from *Snow White and the Seven Dwarfs* of 1937. Walt was intimately involved in the design and construction of the new Studio, pursuing a Utopian vision of a campus for creative work. The creative output generated at this Studio became the linchpin for a whole raft of additional locales and efforts throughout the region. The Studio lot, itself, has been transformed and has grown significantly beyond its initial scope. Additional working spaces were created to house the expanding operations of Walt Disney Productions, as it was then known. These included the campus for WED Enterprises—now known as Walt Disney Imagineering—in the years after the creation of Disneyland. The nondescript warehouses of an industrial park on the site of the former Grand Central Air Terminal in Glendale have been the home base of WDI and other groups since the early 1960s, with many buildings coming and going or undergoing significant renovation.

Many buildings and venues that indicate the influence of the Disney organization can be found throughout the region today. In the heart of Hollywood, one can find the El Capitan Theatre—a grand movie palace that WDI helped to restore and that has since hosted many modern film premieres. It is flanked by Disney's Soda Fountain and Studio Store. In Valencia—to the north and west of the Disney Studio—resides the campus of the California Institute of the Arts, known as CalArts. Walt played a major role in the the development of the school, which was a combination of the Chouinard Art Institute and the Los Angeles Conservatory of Music, and granted the institute the land on which the campus is located. CalArts was one of Walt's major areas of focus in his later years, and the Company still maintains many connections to the school to this day. The nearby Golden Oak Ranch—890 acres of rolling landscape owned by the Company in Canyon Country—has been a key exterior filming location since 1959.

And of course Disneyland is found in the greater Los Angeles area. In theory, Walt could have built Disneyland anywhere. There were many reasons he chose the site that he did, besides the fact that it was near his base of operation. California's ties to the entertainment industry, the phenomenal weather that makes Disneyland such a fantastic year-round destination, and the vibrancy of this part of the country were all part of the allure that convinced Walt that this was where he should build such an endeavor.

A New Vision

Park expansion overview map by Ray Cadd

Everything Walt Disney Imagineering builds is subject to nonstop reevaluation, in order for us to ensure that it remains relevant and valuable for our guests. We constantly change the Parks and other venues, adding and substituting in order to try to present the best show we possibly can. This effort involves input from all parts of our Walt Disney Parks and Resorts business as well as feedback from our guests. However, the amount of change seen at Disney California Adventure between 2007 and 2012 was unprecedented.

The Park was originally envisioned as a counterpoint to Disneyland—a different offering with a distinct tone and selection of experiences intended to provide variety for guests at the resort. But the proximity of Disneyland pointed out that there are elements of the Disney Park experience that Disney California Adventure—in its original incarnation—did not possess. It became clear that for our guests these elements were essential in order to create the connection that they feel to our Parks.

A Disney Park is more than just a disparate series of experiences. It ties these experiences together and connects them to a deeper context that gives a day there greater meaning than just the sum of the parts could provide. It stretches its stories and weaves them into many that our guests know prior to their visits to the Parks. There is an element of reassurance, a connection to the past, and a view to the future, and permission is granted to everybody to see the world like a child again. A Disney Park gives its visitors something to take away with them so that the experience lasts well beyond the Park's gates.

Quick Change

So, when it became clear that Disney California Adventure was not yet striking all of the notes that we want our Parks to hit upon, the Imagineers went back to the drawing board. They worked with our partners in the Parks and Resorts division to fundamentally remake the Park to a degree that had never before been attempted in the history of Disney Parks. A tremendous amount of time, money, and human effort was directed toward building as much additional heart and meaning as possible into the experiences found in the Park. We wanted to ensure that the feelings and memories that a guest left with at the end of a day at Disney California Adventure would resonate for years to come.

Chief amongst the changes, and in many ways the most difficult to achieve, was the reconfiguration of the main entrance and the introduction of Buena Vista Street as the primary statement of purpose for the Park. It establishes why the Park is meaningful to our Company and to our guests. This reconfiguration of the Park's entry sequence set the stage for a new underlying story to support the Park and the experiences contained within. The story tells of a place that exemplifies so many of the shared values of the American people—of optimism, ingenuity, and the pursuit of dreams—and the lure that this land held for a young Walt Disney bent on finding a place to pursue his own dreams and from which to share them with the world.

The rest of the preexisting Park was viewed through this same filter, as was the entire roster of new additions that were considered for the reimagined Disney California Adventure. The story of the resulting Park points toward a bright future for itself and for the unique state that it proudly represents.

The Streamline Moderne spires of the Pan Pacific Auditorium of 1935 create a soaring image welcoming guests into our vision of California as a beacon of forward thinking and the pioneering spirit.

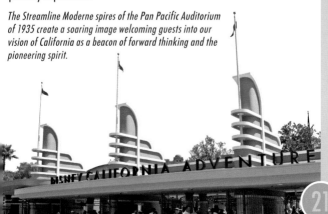

Night Vision

From the earliest days of Walt's preparations for Disneyland, Imagineers have created nighttime bird's-eye renderings of the Parks we are planning to build. These images, which are among the most romantic and anticipatory pieces of art in all of the Imagineering catalog, capture an allure that comes to life at night when the lights come up at all of our Parks around the world. There's something magical about that time of night, as a new energy descends on the Park and brings it to life in a whole new way after dark.

In the case of Disneyland, an early piece of art Walt requested was an aerial shot of the Park by Peter Ellenshaw. This painting was large—covering the entirety of a four-foot-by-eight-foot storyboard. The point of view was chosen because it laid out before viewers all of the wonders they would soon be able to explore. On his Sunday night television show, *Disneyland*, Walt proudly showed off the big surprise; under ultraviolet light the scene changed to night!

A Fantastic Tool of the Trade

In addition to capturing that nighttime magic, these illustrations do several things for us. They give a broad overview of the offerings of a Park, and demonstrate how they will work together. They highlight very clearly where the guest circulation pathways will lay within the overall footprint as they are illuminated against the darker building masses and landscape. And they draw the viewer's focus where we want it to be, on all of the fantastical creations that will make up the Park (and away from all of the necessary infrastructure and back-of-house support).

Overall Park bird's-eye illustration by Tom Gilleon

Lastly, they serve as some of our greatest previews of things to come. Generations of children have stared at these paintings and dreamt of the fun to be had at the finished Park. The Imagineers wanted to foster just this sense of excitement and anticipation about the remaking of Disney California Adventure. There's no better way to convince somebody that this is a place they want to be than with a nighttime bird's-eye. We couldn't wait to get there ourselves!

BUENA VISTA STREET

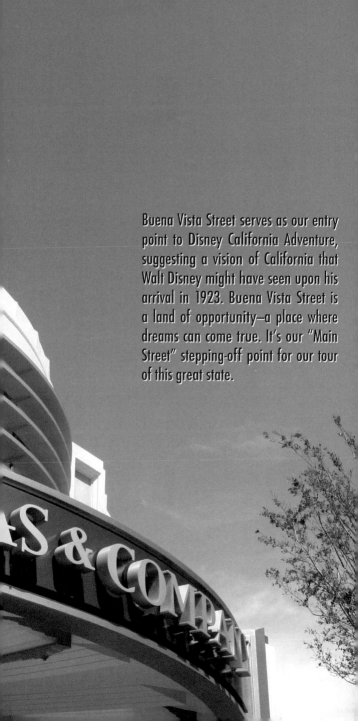

Buena Vista Street serves as our entry point to Disney California Adventure, suggesting a vision of California that Walt Disney might have seen upon his arrival in 1923. Buena Vista Street is a land of opportunity—a place where dreams can come true. It's our "Main Street" stepping-off point for our tour of this great state.

Setting the Scene

Concept sketch of Buena Vista Street entry by Christopher Smith

Now You've Arrived!

Named for the street on which the famed Walt Disney Studios is located, Buena Vista Street marks the entry to Disney California Adventure and is a clear summation of what the Park is about. Like Main Street, U.S.A. at Disneyland, which shows us the memories Walt took from his small-town boyhood, Buena Vista Street presents a welcoming statement that is key to the Park's underlying mythology. Here we get a glimpse of Walt's young adulthood, and the world he might have remembered from his arrival in Los Angeles in 1923, taking full measure of all that California represented to him. Buena Vista Street presents a vital and exciting time and place, where dreams are possible and opportunities are plenty.

Our version of that time and place is not a historical account, but rather an idealized image meant to convey what might have been. Much the way Main Street is not a literal re-creation of the Marceline, Missouri, of Walt's youth, Buena Vista Street pays homage to real places but does not re-create them exactly. It takes inspiration from those reference points and coalesces them into an idea of a place that never truly existed.

Buena Vista Street is a prime example of the way the Park represents California—as a land full of opportunity ripe for the taking. This image of California is what lured Walt and has continued to lure so many other people to California over the years. Buena Vista Street exudes a spirit of optimism that has come to define the state of California in the eyes of the rest of the country. A microcosm of our nation itself, California and its people possess many of the traits that we think of as uniquely American, such as the large, diverse population, the bounty of natural and material resources, and determination on the part of the state's residents to always challenge the status quo and keep moving forward. These are the traits that particularly appealed to Walt, and that drove him to persevere as he strove to get his fledgling enterprise off the ground. His California dreams took shape and took flight and led him to remarkable heights.

You Oughtta Be Making Pictures...

Hollywood in the 1920s was truly seen as a dream factory, full of people from around the United States and around the world who had heard the siren call and had traveled there to make their mark in the world of entertainment. We see this energy represented by the period-style characters and performers on Buena Vista Street. Walt was no different than the composite characters represented by these performers in spirit or ambition, but instead of wanting to become a "star"—as so many of those who had flocked to California in the early days of the budding film industry did—he brought with him grand and original ideas that revolved around pioneering new forms of entertainment.

Name Game

Most of the nomenclature found on Buena Vista Street has ties to the Company's history. In this way, subtle connections are drawn to Walt's early days in Los Angeles and the people, places, and characters who influenced him at that time. As you walk around Buena Vista Street, keep an eye out for the signage placed throughout the land...

• The "California Limited" billboard—destinations in Chicago, Kansas City, and Los Angeles trace Walt's migration west.

• Los Feliz Five & Dime—Walt and Roy once lived in and spent a good amount of time working in the Los Feliz area of Los Angeles.

• Kingswell Camera Shop—Walt and Roy's first actual office was located on Kingswell Avenue in the Silver Lake neighborhood.

• Hollymont Property Associates—a reference to the Holly Vermont Realty Company, with whom the Disneys shared an office in the Kingswell building.

• The "2719 Buena Vista Street" address sign—a reference to the street number of the Hyperion Avenue studio.

• Lessing, Kamen and James, Counselors at Law—Company lawyers.

• Oswald's—a popular Disney character who predated Mickey Mouse.

• Clarabelle's—Clarabelle Cow was a character from early shorts.

• Eye Works Special Optometric Processes—a graphic that acknowledges Ub Iwerks, one of Walt's earliest and most influential collaborators, who was known for his prolific animation of Mickey Mouse, as well as the development of numerous breakthroughs in optical camera techniques.

• Mortimer's Market—in recognition of Walt's original name for Mickey Mouse before Walt's wife, Lillian, convinced him that Mickey was the better name.

The Architecture of Buena Vista Street

Street Scene

Bird's-eye illustration of entry plaza by Victor Post

In order to create a cohesive street with the vibrancy and variety that we wanted to achieve, the team actually assigned individual building facades to different designers. Each worked from the same style guide and references, but was given different program requirements based on the address, and developed his or her own spaces. This way the street feels less contrived and more "organic," as though it came into being naturally over time. Each building presents its own identity, but due to the consistency in the style guide the end result is more cohesive than a streetscape one might have found during the 1920s. The building "lot lines" were also moved around so that each building did not have the same amount of frontage on the street, further avoiding an overly packaged appearance. This type of detail is important, even in an instance in which our goal is not strict historical interpretation but instead the creation of a fictional place that feels *believable* rather than necessarily *realistic*.

The Architecture of Buena Vista Street

BUENA VISTA STREET

Looking Forward by Looking Back

The architectural designers of Buena Vista Street employed many of the same techniques as those used by the designers who have created Main Street, U.S.A. in various Parks over the years. And they've done so with the same intent—to impart a welcoming sensibility and to foster pangs of nostalgia and an emotional connection even within an audience that for the most part has never actually experienced this time or place before. The details that are heightened on Buena Vista Street—the decorative flourishes; the artisanal crafts, such as tile work and art glass; lighting fixtures and other industrial design elements; the exaggeration of cornices; and other defining architectural elements—are the same ones that characterize Main Street, U.S.A. This carefully curated nostalgia is the architectural reassurance upon which Disney Parks are built.

Concept of Carthay Circle fountain plaza by Ray Spencer

QUICK TAKES

• Buena Vista Street most closely represents the Silver Lake and Atwater Village neighborhoods near Hollywood.

• Styles range from Spanish Colonial Revival to Mission Revival to Art Deco, and cover the years between the mid-1890s and the late 1920s.

Color elevation of the Western building block facades

29

Wired

Red Car concept sketch by Chris Turner

The Red Car Trolley is a key part of making Buena Vista Street feel like a different time and place. Even the nonfunctional overhead electrical wiring is part of the look. While in the real world this isn't considered to be an attractive addition to the urban environment, all one has to do is envision the trolley rolling down the street without the wiring to understand how much it contributes to the believability of the scene.

Stairways to Nowhere

A common scenic device used to create the impression that the "world" presented in the Park extends beyond what we literally built is the inclusion of "stairways to nowhere." These elements, along with faux doorways and additional graphics, give a guest the subconscious belief that there's more going on behind those walls than meets the eye. These details have just enough definition to be believable, but not enough to truly draw your attention or distract from the primary elements.

Stairway to nowhere outside the Sepulveda Building

QUICK TAKES

• The music of Buena Vista Street is taken from the big band and dance hall music of the 1920s and 1930s. These selections were made not only for their adherance to the time period of the land, but for the infectious bounce and exuberance that they impart on anyone who hears them. And keep an ear out for the old-time 1930s radio broadcast at Oswald's!

• The music heard in the Carthay Circle Theatre represents classic Disney songs rearranged into period orchestration and recorded specifically for the venue by an ensemble known as The Circle Session Players.

Partners in Storytelling

A companion piece to the *Partners* statue in front of Sleeping Beauty Castle in Disneyland, the *Storytellers* statue in Carthay Circle similarly pays homage to our Company founder and his signature creation, Mickey Mouse. *Storytellers* offers a literal vision of Walt Disney as he might have appeared when he first set foot in California in 1923. The legend says that he arrived with only $40 to his name, but with big ideas about the stories he wanted to tell the world.

The statue was sculpted by Rick Terry, an apprentice of Blaine Gibson, the Disney Legend who set the standard for Disney sculpture for decades, and the one who is responsible for *Partners*.

Walt's suitcase tells us a little about where he has come from. There is a sticker identifying the Laugh-O-Gram Studios, his first business endeavor back in Kansas City. The luggage tag for the Atchison, Topeka and Santa Fe Railroad, shows the claim number 12501, a reference to Walt's December 5th, 1901, birthday.

Storytellers *statue concepts*
by George Scribner

31

Carthay Circle Theatre

Concept illustration of Carthay Circle Theatre by Victor Post

We've Come Full Circle

In the annals of Disney Company history, there are few events as momentous as the 1937 premiere of Walt Disney's first animated feature—*Snow White and the Seven Dwarfs*. This film introduced the world to a new art form, and irrevocably altered the course of the Company's future. As the world fell in love with the characters, Walt was already preparing to tell more and more stories in this exciting new medium. The small fortune that ensued due to the rampant success of *Snow White* paved the way for the Disney brothers to construct the new Walt Disney Studios in Burbank, and set the Company off on the path toward becoming the world-renowned entertainment entity that it is today.

The venue for *Snow White*'s grand premiere is equally storied in Company lore, in part because it has long since disappeared. From its debut in 1926 to its demolition in 1969, the Carthay Circle Theatre—by architects Carleton Winslow and Dwight Gibbs—hosted several major motion picture premieres. A vision in white with its Spanish Colonial Revival style, the theater's striking, octagonal tower and sweeping parapets, evocative of a circus tent, were visible from far away in the Los Angeles of its heyday, and served as a glamorous symbol of the booming movie business in Southern California.

The theater's import in both Hollywood and Disney history makes it a fitting centerpiece for Disney California Adventure, and its classic design makes for an inviting vista as seen from the entrance of the Park.

A Little Taste of History

Our Carthay Circle Theatre holds different activities within its confines than did the original venue. There is no theater proper, as there was no need for that in the Park. The greater need was to allow guests to truly experience a bit of the time and place that the land is intended to call forth. So the Imagineering team developed three distinct dining and lounge venues within our structure. The ground floor Carthay Circle Lounge and private 1901 Club, and the Carthay Circle Restaurant upstairs, evoke the glamour days of Hollywood, and the types of places in which the show business elite would gather. In addition, 1901 also evokes a little bit of Disneyland. The club, named after the year of Walt Disney's birth, is a companion to his private Club 33 that resides on the second story of the buildings of Disneyland's New Orleans Square.

Carthay Circle Restaurant concept by Ray Spencer and Anastasia Pavlova

QUICK TAKES

•Imagineering built a much smaller replica of the Carthay Circle Theatre on Sunset Boulevard at Disney's Hollywood Studios in Florida.

•The lounge and the restuarant share a soundtrack, but with different instrumentations to make the lounge livelier and the restaurant more elegant. The two are in sync so that when one passes from one space to the other the transition is seamless.

•The original Carthay Circle Theatre was located at the intersection of San Vicente Boulevard and McCarthy Vista in the Carthay residential development in the Mid-City West neighborhood of Los Angeles.

•Three years after *Snow White*, the theater hosted the Los Angeles premiere of *Fantasia*, for which the remarkable "Fantasound" audio system was installed, at Walt Disney's insistence.

CONDOR FLATS

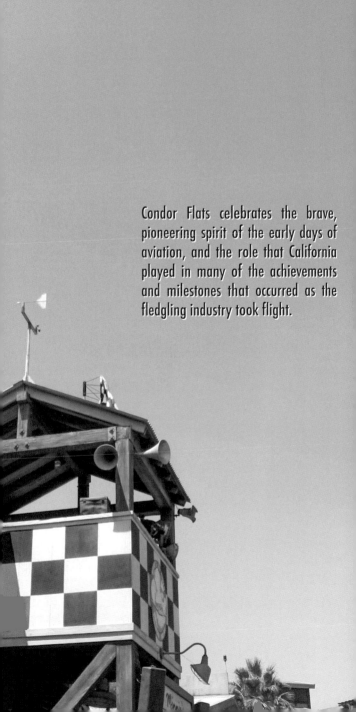

Condor Flats celebrates the brave, pioneering spirit of the early days of aviation, and the role that California played in many of the achievements and milestones that occurred as the fledgling industry took flight.

Early Condor Flats concept by Tim Delaney

Up, Up, and Away...

Condor Flats is dedicated to the importance of California in the early days of the burgeoning aerospace industry. Determined people took to challenging places like the Mojave Desert to test the limits of man's abilities. Their ingenuity, paired with feats of derring-do, led to some of the key advances that created modern aviation as we know it today.

Remnants of runways, hangars, garages, and engines take us back to a place where the sky was most definitely *not* the limit. The signal lights and wind socks and the racing cars being prepped for speed runs on the salt flats clue us in as to what kinds of things go on in Condor Flats and what type of people would be found doing them. The land serves as a loving homage to the fearless exploration that made our world just a little bit smaller.

A Very Important Time

The focus on aviation, and the major events that shaped its development, show up in a display inside the Fly 'n' Buy shop. The calendar is marked off to the date of October 14, 1947. The clock is stopped at 10:27 to correspond to the exact time at which famed test pilot Chuck Yeager broke the sound barrier in flight for the first time. This clock was presumably stopped by the sonic boom that ensued!

Soarin' facade color elevation by Amy Henderson

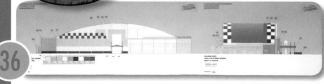

Study Comes First

Land entry concept sketch by Ray Spencer

These two images (above and below) by WDI designer Ray Spencer demonstrate the ways in which an illustration can evolve as work progresses. Often a sketch precedes a more finished illustration. Even in an instance in which the general point of view and subject matter remains the same, you can see that detail elements and fine points of the illustration can change from one pass to the next.

Land entry concept illustration by Ray Spencer

Condor Flats aerial view by Ray Spencer

Soarin' Over California

Conceptual sketch of Soarin' experience by Ray Spencer

A Real Bird's-Eye View

One of the most notable features of the state of California is its gorgeous geography and scenery. It's one of our largest states and counts among its many environments a beautiful coastline, majestic and even snow-capped mountains, hearty farmland, strikingly beautiful deserts, peaceful forests, national parks, and exciting urban cityscapes. The amazing variety and spectacular grandeur of the vistas that can be found by traversing the state can truly take one's breath away.

These attributes, combined with the Condor Flats backstory of aviation led to the development of Soarin' Over California, a fantastic flight from one end of the Golden State to the other. Aided by a smooth and silent ride mechanism, the attraction allows guests to glide into position so that they can be fully enveloped in the world on-screen to support the notion of flying. The engineering effort required to achieve this seamless result is important to our staging of the show. Take note of how smoothly and quietly you're moved into position when the lights go down. The silent mechanism, developed specifically for this show by WDI engineers, is a marvel of simplicity and unobtrusive operation. It avoids any outside sensory interference that can pull an audience out of the show.

The effect of immersion is heightened by the inclusion of additional sensory inputs such as the smell of a pine forest and the feel of the wind blowing on your face. The seats move gently to indicate changes in your direction of flight, and the theater itself is enhanced to project the audience as fully into the scene as possible.

These conceptual images by Ray Spencer demonstrate the concept of how the attraction functions. When we develop these new ideas, we have to communicate them in a way that allows the viewer to

see clearly how this new thing will work. Part of the challenge for the concept designer is to choose the point of view and determine which elements to include that will make the communication clearly readable.

QUICK TAKES

• The iconic musical score for Soarin' Over California was created for the attraction by motion picture composer Jerry Goldsmith.

• Imagineer Mark Sumner came up with the solution to the particularly vexing engineering challenge of the Soarin' ride system while playing with an old Erector set. He created a working model at home over a weekend. Sometimes we take our work home with us literally, but we're always thinking about the work we do and looking for better ways to accomplish what we're trying to achieve—whether that takes the form of a new creative development or a novel technical approach.

Concept for the entry corridor by Ray Spencer

A Pointed Statement

The residents of a planter bed in Condor Flats

When we design an area meant to tell a given story, any and all elements are in play as a means to reinforce that story. Landscape design is certainly a major part of that. The plant selection on an attraction like Jungle Cruise at Disneyland or Kilimanjaro Safaris at Disney's Animal Kingdom is key to transporting you to those exotic places. But even in a story setting a little bit closer to home like Condor Flats, the plants can tell us quite a bit. In this case, the plants aren't chosen only for their geographical accuracy, but also to impart a sense of the harshness of the environment in which these pioneers of aviation chased their dreams into the sky. The sharp tips at the end of a frond on a century plant or the many needles of a prickly pear cactus tell the viewer in a single glance that this is not a place in which things come easily. The accuracy of the environment is important, but keep in mind that there are also reasons one chooses to tell a particular story in a particular setting.

Overall land concept by Ray Spencer

Flyover Storytelling

Sometimes it's easy to *underlook* the things that are going on right over our heads. Don't miss the propping and set dressing in the Fly 'n' Buy merchandise shop in Condor

Flats. Make sure to look up into the high bay in the garage to see the signs of the motor-heads who work here gearing up for another speed run on the salt flats. And don't miss the fact that the point-of-sale is built into the garage's tool crib. These are the ways designers use backstories to flesh out their designs in ways that make sense.

A Cool Coincidence

One thing you want when you design a place that's about flight and space exploration is a big rocket engine. And one thing you need when you design a station that's supposed to spray cooling mist on guests as they make their way through the Park is a big nozzle. If you keep your mind open to finding these connections, you find yourself doing some Imagineering.

EUREKA

GOLD AND TIMBER CO

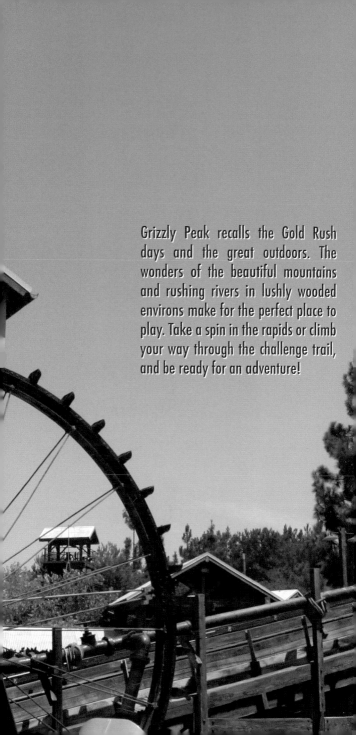

Grizzly Peak recalls the Gold Rush days and the great outdoors. The wonders of the beautiful mountains and rushing rivers in lushly wooded environs make for the perfect place to play. Take a spin in the rapids or climb your way through the challenge trail, and be ready for an adventure!

Grizzly Peak overall aerial concept illustration by Ned Mueller

Fun in the Sun

California has always been known for its plentiful recreational offerings that take advantage of the great outdoors. The diversity of its natural settings in which to play is broader than that of many countries. There are mountains and forests and beaches and streams. There are many national and state parks, with Yosemite National Park being one of the best known in the nation. Grizzly Peak pays homage to this bounty of natural environments and gives us all an excuse to go play for a bit.

From the raucous splashdown of Grizzly River Run to the challenge of Redwood Creek, this land is all about the outdoors and the adventures to be found there. The guest in this land plays the role of a Californian out for an excursion or of one of the many visitors who come to experience the state's bounty for themselves. Yosemite itself draws around four million people a year. Clearly in a man-made setting like this, there is no way to re-create the majestic splendor of a real place like one of those parks, so our goals here are to capture the essence of the experience—the connection with nature, the visceral delights of the splashing waters and the trees blowing in the breeze, and the rustic charm of the places found in California—so that our guests might be inspired to go see the real thing!

Historical markers like this one placed in the land allow us to share background information with our guests in a way that is completely organic to the national park setting of Grizzly Peak. This gives the Park additional value as a place to learn, while further reinforcing our placemaking.

Leading the Way

Yosemite is not only one of the best-known national parks in the nation. It played a crucial role in the development of the entire National Park Service system. In 1864, a bill was signed by President Abraham Lincoln to create the Yosemite Grant—the first time the federal government had ever acted to preserve land for public use. This precedent led the way, eight years later, to the establishment of Yellowstone as the first of the national parks and the launching pad for the park service. It is this significant piece of California history and the role played by the state in an important movement within our entire country that makes this setting a meaningful addition to the menu of offerings in Disney California Adventure. This context takes the meaning of this land beyond merely being a fantastic place to go outside and play.

Grizzly Peak cuts a distinctive figure.

UICK TAKES

• Grizzly Peak itself is 110 feet high.

• The mountain represents the form of a California grizzly—also known as a California golden bear—which is the state animal of California.

• Grizzly Peak is not intended to represent Yosemite or any other particular national park, but rather to serve as a composite representing all of the parks and the overall natural beauty of the state.

Watercolor study sketch of Grizzly Peak by Tom Gilleon

A Raft of Fun

Grizzly River Rapids splashdown sketch by Topper Helmers.

The marquee attraction of Grizzly Peak is Grizzly River Run—a rip-roarin' ride running rapidly 'round the rivers and streams of this outdoor wonderland. Voice-over announcements in the queue, set dressing along the river's banks, and propping arrangements throughout all work together to tell you about the former function of this place. Our back-story tells us of a past legacy of gold and timber mining—predating our contemporary awareness of the need to preserve such pristine places—and of this mining site's subsequent conversion into a recreation outfitter and guide company. This layering of historical elements gives us the tool set we use to carry out our designs and construct the framework against which to test our decisions along the way. Our goals are to create as much fun as possible for our guests, hence spewing geysers, leaking waterways, swales and waves, and of course the big splashdown drop!

The "old" waterwheel of the Eureka Gold and Timber Co. appears to send the raft ascending toward the top of Grizzly Peak

Grizzly River Run concept elevation by Chris Runco

UICK TAKES

•Take note of the initials for Grizzly River Run and it just might give you a clue as to what you should keep an eye out for in the forests of Grizzly Peak.

•Elevated water trough rides such as Grizzly River Run require a reservoir into which the water is diverted whenever the attraction is not in operation. Here, due to the limited space available around the mountain owing to the fact that is surrounded on all sides by guest areas, the design team had to be very resourceful. The tide pools on the front of the Pacific Wharf area are used as the repository for the water from our flume, adding show value to the Park while also serving a very important function. The volume was precisely balanced to ensure that water levels would be just right when the rafts were running.

•Don't be concerned by the apparent leaks you see in the side of the sluice over the top of the main drop. Those are not really failures in the integrity of the structure, but are rather the handiwork of our Special Effects team—ensuring that if you haven't gotten wet by that point that you soon will!

Grizzly River Run sketch by Chris Runco

Redwood Creek Challenge Trail bird's-eye illustration by Chuck Ballew

A Challenging Design

Everybody loves to play. Imagineers love to play! But Imagineers also like to create play spaces for others. As design exercises, play spaces in the Disney Parks bring challenges and opportunities that are truly unique. These spaces must clear all of the same hurdles as any of our other design efforts—they have to be part of our cohesive show, they have to connect to the spaces around them, they have to be durable—and they also must connect with guests. They must allow for an appropriate number of guests to pass through, while engaging them all in ways that are interesting, fun, safe, active, and often interactive. Our play spaces must accommodate children of different ages and abilities and typically the adults who accompany them, and must fill our younger guests with a sense of accomplishment. They should foster exploration, allow for a bit of energy to be burnt off, and leave kids wanting to come back for more. These types of attractions present us with our own kind of challenge!

Redwood Creek concept sketch by Bob Barrett

A Story by Any Other Name...

It's often said that everything we do at Imagineering is about story—and it is. But that phrase in and of itself is really just shorthand for a much more nuanced idea of what "story" means in our medium of Disney Parks. It doesn't mean the same thing that it would mean if we were writing a book, making a movie, drawing a comic strip, or even standing on a stage telling a story to an audience. None of those media are approached in exactly the same way by the creators in those fields, so why would we expect that this one wouldn't follow its own path?

The meaning of "story" is also very different depending on whether we are talking about a Park, a land, an attraction, a restaurant, a resort, a water park, a game, a shopping district, a theater, a playground, a cruise ship, or any number of other experiences we may develop. Each of these carries with it a very different sensibility around the idea of "story." The delivery mechanisms are unique to each venue. The degree of agency—or control over the course of events—on the part of the guest varies. The ratio of narrative plot explication versus experiential storytelling can fall anywhere along a very broad spectrum. The goals for the experience vary on the part of the Imagineers and of the guests.

Disney Parks are really more like storytelling environments—designed in much the same way a film set might be. The difference is that here a series of locations, situations, and experiences is presented to a guest who has the freedom to choose where to look, where to walk, in what order to experience the offerings of the Park, and a number of other variables. We can't control the "camera" the way a film director can, which means that the guest is a key collaborator in creating these "stories." For example, in a pedestrian area of the Park, we tend to put guests into an environment in which story is imparted through the design of spaces and the elements within those spaces. Backstory is told via sensory evidence that something *has happened*; the show we overlay to this may include things that *are happening*, and the guest then anticipates or even participates in the story that *will happen*. The Park, then, is really just a place where stories can happen.

In an attraction, where we have control over a guest's movements through the scenes, those scenes play out in an order of our choosing. But even this does not mean that a narrative story arc with a beginning, a middle, and an end is necessarily the goal. There is not always a plot, per se. Some attractions—including some of our most popular—revolve more around sequential experiences connected by ideas. But these still fall under our broad definition of "story."

Grizzly Peak sketch by Jerry Bingham

Bear-ly Visible

Grizzly Peak watercolor sketches by Tom Gilleon

It is a tricky proposition to design an animal character into a "natural" rock formation in a way that is believable. For Grizzly Peak itself, it was very important that the namesake bear in the mountain be apparent to the eye, but not too over*bear*ing in the overall scene. This led to a great deal of development art in which different poses, compositions, and rockwork styles were tried out so that we could make some determinations to dictate the rockwork modeling effort. The end result is an icon that is one of the most recognizable symbols of the Park.

Sign Define

The walking path that runs between the lands of Condor Flats and the neighboring Grizzly Peak very subtly sets up the story of our national park backdrop through the placement of roadside informational signs like those that would be found on a typical drive through the woods to a place like the Grizzly Peak Recreation Area.

Crafty Design

The lamps, railings, and fixtures in Grizzly Peak take on a Craftsman character in order to transition well from the adjacent Grand Californian Hotel. This relationship is one reason Grizzly Peak was sited where it was during the Park's development.

QUICK TAKES

•While in reality our Grizzly Peak measures 110 feet tall, the scenic map of nearby peaks in Rushin' River Outfitters credits it as being 2,001 feet, as a reference to the Park's 2001 opening date.

•The Eureka Gold and Timber Company takes its name from the state motto of California.

As Scene on the Edge of the River

Sometimes the little details placed around the Park tell a story of their own. The remnants of the steam donkey operation visible across the creek from the scenic overlook next to the Eureka waterwheel gives us a clear sense of the origins of this place, due to the nature of the propping and the antique elements. The setting tells us what's going on here—an abandoned mining and logging operation predating the current national park—giving us a sense of the history of this part of the state. It's up to the Park guest to fill in the blanks and imagine what may unfold next in this story we create together every day.

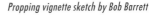

Propping vignette sketch by Bob Barrett

PARADISE PIER

Paradise Pier is a vision of a California seaside amusement pier that never truly existed. It's an idealized take on the boardwalks and midways that entertained many Californians of the 1920s in waterfront parks at beaches all along the Pacific coast.

Inspirational image for Paradise Pier by Anastasia Pavlova

Piering into the Past

Paradise Pier captures some of the fun of California in the 1920s by evoking the spirit of the classic seaside amusement boardwalks and pleasure piers that used to dot the Pacific coastline from San Francisco to San Diego. Most of these landmarks have long since vanished, but they remain a part of our collective memories of the state. While in many ways these piers evolved into something that was the antithesis of what Walt wanted to create with Disneyland, here we celebrate the origins of these places and the nostalgic, idealized image of them that has survived well beyond the life span of most of the parks themselves.

These venues offered, in their day, the height of thrills (sometimes literally) in the burgeoning amusement park industry. Adventurous park-goers were treated to the latest inventions intended to excite and even frighten them, with attractions running the full spectrum from carousels to fun houses, and Ferris wheels to roller coasters. Our Paradise Pier includes many of those same items, with unique nods to modernity that take the experience to places the old amusement pier proprietors could never have imagined.

Boardwalk overall color elevation

The Old Stuff Is the New Stuff

As part of the Park's makeover, Paradise Pier was redressed to feature more of the Victorian detailing that lent the charm to classic amusement parks. These details cement in our guests' eyes the more romantic, heightened-reality version of the reality that we want to celebrate.

Paradise Pier logo graphic design

QUICK TAKES

• The heyday for these classic amusement piers was the 1920s, right around the time of Walt's arrival in California.

• Many of the pleasure piers were built by transplanted East Coasters looking to re-create the Coney Island-type parks from back home.

Paradise Pier boardwalk concept by Christopher Smith

Concept sketch by Larry Nikolai, Chris Merritt, and Anastasia Pavlova

Under the Scene

The Little Mermaid is recognized as one of the most beloved Disney animated features of all time, and as the harbinger of the second Golden Age of Disney Animation that saw the art form's resurgence through the late 1980s and 1990s. The charming (or in some cases villainous) characters, the memorable songs, and the fantastic animation all added up to a film experience that fans have gone back to time and time again since its debut in 1989. All of those same ingredients make *The Little Mermaid* a prime candidate for the Disney Park treatment, as well. The opportunity to take guests under the sea to see this world unfold around them and to re-create some of the best-known scenes from the film was something the Imagineers had hoped to take advantage of for many years. In this application, the attraction is a perfect fit for Paradise Pier, in that it stands in as our version of the old fun house rides that were the precursor to the modern dark ride. Ours of course employs all that we have learned in half a century of creating this sort of attraction, and shows what those early examples have evolved into.

Attraction load mural by Larry Nikolai

Good Ideas Never Go Out to Pasture—or Out to Sea...

The Imagineers had been looking for the right time and place to build an attraction based on this film for some time. There have been ideas pursued in other Parks and with different show formats many times over the years. But in order for us to move forward with an idea, no matter how much we may like it, many factors all have to align to make it a good fit for the entire Company. However, we never stop looking for a place for a good idea. In this case, Paradise Pier represented the perfect landing spot for Ariel on this coast, while the concurrent New Fantasyland development at Magic Kingdom features a very similar iteration of the attraction, but with a very different queue and load structure that makes that one live properly in its land.

QUICK TAKES

- There are more than 170 animated figures in nine show scenes.

- Ursula is one of the largest and most complicated Audio-Animatronics figures ever in a Disney dark ride.

- The Little Mermaid~Ariel's Undersea Adventure works very well to represent the Art Nouveau references within our treatment of Paradise Pier. Its winding seaweed forms and other flowing shapes all play well within the graceful, organic vernacular that Art Nouveau is known for.

Scuttle sketch by Chris Merritt

57

Goofy's Sky School concept by Jim Shull

A Fly into the Wall

Continuing the theme of connecting the attractions in the Park, whenever possible, to the Company's heritage, Goofy's Sky School came to Paradise Pier in the form of a wacky roller coaster on which you never know what near miss is going to befall you next. The attraction captures the spirit of a Goofy "How to..." short, in which Goofy's well-intentioned attempt to assist and instruct us on a particular task quickly goes awry and leads to all manner of high jinks. The subject this time around is flying, and Goofy certainly fancies himself a master aviator! If only his flying were a match for his winning confidence.

The Imagineering team set about the task of developing this new attraction in just the same way a team of animators would set out to make a short film. After first establishing their premise, or the central scenario that would become the framework upon which to hang their "gags," they begin cranking out idea after idea to add to that through line and bring the humor into the mix. In this case that meant a lot of funny results due to Goofy's lack of flying skills.

58

The Gag Session

When creating a new attraction, the story team collaboratively discusses the "rules of the game," as they have established them, for the story at hand. They throw jokes and sketches at one another, looking to see which ones will elicit a response. Those jokes may end up in the final show verbatim, or they may simply serve as a launching pad for another variation on that joke or an entirely different one that it inspires. The designers do drawings to show how a particular gag would play out visually, and the team discusses whether there is a better way to communicate the intent. Eventually the team arrives at the final slate, and that is put into further development.

Nighttime concept sketch by Anastasia Pavlova

QUICK TAKES

• Goofy's Sky School was formerly known as Mulholland Madness, a madcap ride on Mulholland Drive, the famed Hollywood roadway.

• Designers took some of their inspiration from the 1940 short, *Goofy's Gliders.*

• This type of coaster, known as a "wild mouse," with its twisty un-banked turns, was a staple at classic boardwalk parks like the one portrayed by Paradise Pier.

Inspirational gag sketches for Goofy's Sky School by George Scribner

59

Jumpin' Jellyfish

Conceptual elevation of Jumpin' Jellyfish by Yu Liming

What Goes Up Must Come Down…and Look Pretty

Sometimes the story behind an attraction is more of a stylistic overlay that makes it work within its surrounding context. In this case, the fluid forms of jellyfish and their surrounding stalks of seaweed were thought to be a good complement to both the supposed seaside setting of Paradise Pier and the Art Deco and Art Nouveau stylings of portions of the land derived from the time period it represents. Once designers receive drawings from the engineers and ride designers, they go to work applying the shapes and forms they want to see in ways that shroud the portions of the apparatus that we don't want to see and accent the portions we do. See how the seaweed wrap that spirals around the supporting towers breaks the strong vertical lines of the heavy supporting pipe and softens the mechanism. The points of interest—the carriages with the guests in them—receive the brightest color and the most distinctive shapes and become the focal point of the design. Additional elements in the surrounding area development are designed so as to tie the composition together.

Guests fly high over Paradise Pier aboard the Jumpin' Jellyfish.

Silly Symphony Swings concept elevation by Jim Shull and Anastasia Pavlova

Swing Song

Silly Symphony Swings took over for the original Orange Stinger in a 2010 redressing of the attraction. The ride was originally surrounded by a giant, spiraling orange peel motif that was stripped away—so as to return greater visibility to Paradise Bay and the surrounding areas—and replaced with a scenic and graphic overlay that plays into the swirling, twirling, madcap mayhem of the swings. Here the backdrop recalls the classic animated short *The Band Concert*, from 1935. In the film, Mickey plays the conductor of a small band trying to perform in a park, an effort that gets sidetracked by the onslaught of a tornado that lifts them up and around as they try with all their might to continue following Mickey's feverish commands. You can see the story of the film played out in a series of panels set into the decorative frieze around the edge of the canopy portion of the spinner.

The Band Concert *story panel by Mark Page*

The view to Paradise Pier as night falls

Technically Enlightening

One of the distinguishing features of the old-time amusement piers—some of which were referred to as "Electric Parks"—was the magical way that they lit up at night. The stories of Walt, as a boy, watching the lights come on at Electric Park in Kansas City with his sister Ruth indicate how much of an impression this wonderment left on him. So Paradise Pier lights up magically at night, as well, but with a modern twist. Wherever possible, our lighting designers look for energy-efficient alternatives to traditional lamps, so many of the lights you see in Paradise Pier are LED or other high-efficiency options. The trick is in getting the color temperatures to recall the warmth and enchantment of that bygone era.

Sound Design

These very large speakers, which are required to support the area BGM and to give audio coverage for the World of Color show, are hidden behind decorative screens on the facade of the show building for The Little Mermaid~Ariel's Undersea Adventure. In this way, the speakers are transformed into attractive elements that improve the look of the building while also supporting the technical requirements of the show. We often look for ways to use elements like this to plus the show.

Heights of Reality!

As with most of our design work for the Parks, the look of Paradise Pier was created with poetic license in order to capture the essence of the old amusement parks without replicating them. To that end, the colors are a little more playful, the lines a little softer, the graphics a little richer, and the attitude a little sweeter. These departures from reality are especially important in Paradise Pier in order to maintain

separation between our boardwalk and the real ones. This differentiation allows us to focus our guests' attention on the positive, nostalgic aspects of the historical parks rather than any negative associations.

Cross-Referential

When creating a world in which a given land of a Park is set, we have to think in terms of how this sort of a world might operate. Within a real boardwalk setting such as this, one would find advertisements for various establishments each vying for your patronage. This type of environmental detail is key to making the land feel believable, but it also allows us to create a connectivity within the area that reinforces the guest's understanding of the individual elements and how they interrelate. It creates a world within a world.

Billboard for Boardwalk Pizza & Pasta

Color elevation of California Screamin' and Toy Story Midway Mania!

Fast-Track Design

One of the attractions in Paradise Pier that brings a new twist to an old amusement pier classic is California Screamin', our take on a beachside roller coaster. Instead of a wooden coaster that would have been typical of this sort of a 1920s park, ours has a steel frame made to mimic the appearance of a wooden one. This allows California Screamin' to look the part, while offering the advantages of modern tracks, including the smoothness and physical capabilities that come with a twenty-first century computer-designed engineering effort. Our coaster has loops, tight turns, and an accelerated launch, which an old wooden coaster just wouldn't have been able to handle.

(REALLY) QUICK TAKES

- California Screamin' features 5,577 feet of track, or 1.06 miles.

- The linear induction launch system—in which a series of magnets is activated in sequence in order to accelerate the 17,700 pound coaster trains rapidly toward the initial ascent—takes riders from 0–55 miles per hour in just 4.0 seconds.

- California Screamin' was one of our first roller coasters designed with the assistance of computer pre-visualization, which allowed the team to *experience* the ride well before it was built on-site.

Color elevation of Mickey's Fun Wheel

'll Throw You for a Loop!

e world's first Ferris wheel made its debut in 1893 as one of the
adliners of the World Columbian Exposition in Chicago, a massive
ir built in part by Walt Disney's father, Elias, who worked on-site as
carpenter. Since then, Ferris wheels have sprung up throughout the
orld in ever-increasing sizes.

ur new *spin* on the traditional Ferris wheel is the 160-foot-tall Mickey's
n Wheel, which gives guests two options for how much thrill they
ant to take on. As on the Coney Island Wonder Wheel which inspired
eight of the cabs follow a familiar course around the circumference
the wheel, while sixteen of them offer the additional excitement
traversing loop paths within the overall perimeter. The face on the
heel recalls the title cards of early Mickey Mouse shorts.

e 2009 redevelopment of the Fun Wheel (formerly the Sun Wheel)
cluded the installation of a major show lighting overlay. These lights
d the associated control capabilities not only dress up the attraction
night, but also allow it to serve as something of a preshow, as well as
active backdrop for the World of Color show every night. The 10,880
odules of six LEDs each are placed throughout the armature of
e wheel and are driven by 16,609 control channels, which run
em through a twenty-nine minute show cycle.

65

Attraction posters for Luigi's Flying Tires, The Little Mermaid ~ Ariel's Underse Adventure, and the Red Car Trolley by Greg Maler

The Return of an Old Friend

In striving to ensure that Disney California Adventure would feel mor like the Disney Park that our guests expected it to be, the team looke to some of the touchstones that had defined the Disneyland experienc over the years. One of those treasured elements has always bee the attraction posters that have decorated the tunnels beneath th train station at that Park's entrance. These images have symbolize our old favorites, introduced new additions to the Park, and eve built anticipation for upcoming projects since the earliest days of th Park's existence. There had bee some posters developed for Disne California Adventure over th years, but it became an area c focus for the redevelopmen The team knew that a poste program could set the ton for the communication of th design intent of the Park. S many of the new addition and modifications to the Par were previewed by poster which served to describe th new attractions, and to g people excited about th changes that were coming

Poster art for Flik's Fun Fair by Nicole Armitage

66

No Such Thing As "Typical"

A study of attraction posters developed for Disneyland and subsequent Disney Parks over the years reveals them to be wonderful reflections of the time and place in which the posters were created. The graphic stylings have evolved, the illustrative techniques have changed with the times, the compositions have been quite varied, and the typography has been all over the map! The only characteristics that the posters share are as follows: they strive to capture the spirit of their subject matter; they tend to generally describe the experience at hand; and they attempt to generate excitement for that experience.

The design of a poster oftentimes has more to do with the date the art was produced than the era embodied in the attraction or experience being presented. Posters from the 1950s through today can often be dated within a reasonable range of years based on signature design cues.

For the new Disney California Adventure posters, the team wanted to recapture the essence of some of the earliest Disneyland examples—so as to strengthen the connections to that Park—but with a contemporary

Radiator Springs Racers poster by Greg Maletic

flair that takes advantages of the modern tools of digital design and typesetting. The end result is a hybrid that bridges the design styles of the origins of Disneyland Resort and the new identity of this Park next door.

Posters for Mickey's Fun Wheel and Silly Symphony Swings by Greg Maletic, and The Twilight Zone Tower of Terror™ by Richard Broderick

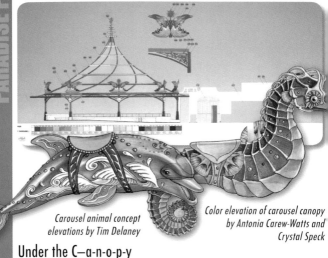

Carousel animal concept elevations by Tim Delaney

Color elevation of carousel canopy by Antonia Carew-Watts and Crystal Speck

Under the C–a-n-o-p-y

Another classic midway attraction is the carousel, which has certainly been featured in Disney Parks since the very beginning. But for Disney California Adventure, instead of finding and renovating an existing vintage specimen, as had been done for the carousels in Disneyland and Magic Kingdom, the Imagineers designed a new one from scratch. It's a whimsical version of a traditional carousel, with motifs recalling both the animated subject matter *revolving* around King Triton from *The Little Mermaid,* and stylized Art Deco-flavored period examples.

Imagineers designed all manner of underwater creatures in a playful and ornate style, combining disparate influences into a cohesive look. With calliope versions of the songs from the film, lights that come on at night, and a distinctive open-air canopy, this carousel is truly a magical experience for riders of all ages.

The stylized dolphins and sea horses, along with Art Deco waveforms and sunbursts, make this carousel a unique visual statement on Paradise Pier.

Concept sketches for Casey at the Bat, Goofy About Fishing, and Bullseye Stallion Stampede, with line work by Ray Cadd and color by John Dickenson

Step Right Up!

On our Paradise Pier, even the humble midway game receives an extra layer of fun. Each of these timeworn staples of the boardwalk was given a story overlay based on a classic Disney animation reference. The activities required by the games themselves inspired the integration of story beats from animated shorts or scenes from feature films. This type of conceptual linkage represents one of the staples of Imagineering, as well. One of the exercises we find ourselves going through quite often is the search for an abstract connection between a story and an action. The catalog of films and characters is reviewed, brainstorming sessions lead to concept development, and in the end we present an idea to intertwine a reference point from one medium into a new one. So, throwing a ball to the catcher recalls *Casey at the Bat*, spraying water at a target leads to putting out the fire in Dumbo's circus, Goofy is the perfect fishin' partner, and Bullseye becomes the ideal foil for a midway horse race!

Paint elevations for Dumbo's Bucket Brigade by Wesley Keil

Golden Zephyr appears in a Paradise Pier rendering by Nicole Armitage

Up, Up, and Around!

Golden Zephyr recalls the fantastic science fiction film serials of the 1930s and 1940s. This form of attraction, known as a Circle Swing, was a fixture at many of the most fondly remembered boardwalks of the 1920s through the 1940s. The gleaming Art Deco styling and free-swinging nature of the gondolas puts you in your own spaceship flying high over Paradise Pier. This design motif represents a past vision of the future that still holds its appeal. These same serial films have served as inspirations for many of the greatest filmmakers of the modern era, and also as reference for the 1994 update of Tomorrowland in Magic Kingdom Park in Florida.

Golden Zephyr concept elevation by Yu Liming

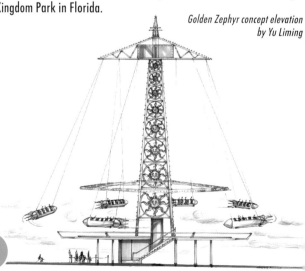

Seeing into the Future

In order to put our best effort into turning dreams into reality, Imagineers are always on the lookout for new tools to add to our tool belt. We keep up with developments in various industries that can be applied to the work we do, and sometimes even develop our own unique tools to allow us to do things that most other types of design and construction groups do not. Modern advances in computer-aided design, modeling, and animation have been a tremendous boon to our process, and allow us to see the things we intend to build far sooner and much more completely than ever before.

We still tend to begin with pencil on paper, and we still build physical models for all the same reasons we have in the past. In recent years, however, our design development processes have been irrevocably altered and improved. Contemporary modeling and drafting applications allow us to build virtual models very quickly and to do most of our design in 3-D from the beginning, and new time-based visualization tools combine our project schedules with the building model so that we can see it all come together before we ever get out to the site. With these tools, we are able to detect and resolve conflicts between various building systems or elements and plan for any logistical challenges that will be encountered during construction.

We also make extensive use of computer-generated imagery to experience a space or an attraction in a virtual manner from a guest's perspective. We have created for ourselves large-format projection environments that allow us to ride the attractions, walk the sites, and look around corners just as a guest would—all within the confines of our design studios. As with any design exercise, the more information we have to influence our efforts, the better.

Computer model of Goofy's Sky School

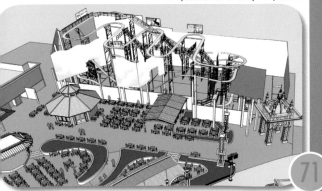

Toy Story Midway Mania!

Concept for Mr. Potato Head as barker by Ray Cadd and Tracey Carpente

Toys and Games

Interactivity gets a new spin with Toy Story Midway Mania!, a frolickin ride through the toy-size world of Andy's bedroom from the Disney•Pixa film *Toy Story*. The Imagineers worked with our colleagues at Pixar t develop a story line that would allow us to bring the film's presence int Disney California Adventure in a big way. In the attraction's story, th toys have opened up a new addition to Andy's collection—a box full o Midway Games—and have wasted no time in playing with them. They'v invited us in to be toys for the day and join in the fun.

The attraction revolves around the notion of taking guests through series of spaces that are essentially life-size video games. 3-D glasse bring the games to life and make the targets pop off the screen, whil rendering each of the projectiles "fired" from our spring-action shooter so that they appear to be traveling away from us and into each scene The games come to life as updated versions of classic Midway Game hosted by Toy Story characters, with each game involving a differen type of object being thrown from guests' shooters toward the variou targets. The three-dimensional effect and the playful animation mak for an engaging and immersive experience.

Much work went into the development of the spring-action shooter t make sure that it would provide adequate feedback for game play whil also holding up to the rigors of daily usage by thousands of guests o a moving ride system. Many mock-ups and much testing of the cabl the guests pull to activate the shooter led to a change in materials t prevent fraying over time. The play-testing process employed by our interactive design group is very important in both hardwar and software development.

Can You Hit the Side of a Barn?

The game logic for Toy Story Midway Mania! was built with the intent of leveling the playing field for players of varying skill levels, in order to maintain the fun for all. The system offers up simpler targets for those whose results indicate that they need a little help, and more difficult targets for those who have proven themselves to be crack shots. The early target practice gives guests a chance to get ready for the challenge, and then the early results begin to affect the difficulty level. It's the only way we've found to give parents a fair shake against the kids!

Toy Story Midway Mania! facade color elevation

QUICK TAKES

• This attraction was built simultaneously in two of our Parks—Disney's Hollywood Studios and Disney California Adventure—a first for us.

• The spring-action shooter is an evolution of a design developed to fire the cannonballs at Pirates of the Caribbean: Battle for Buccaneer Gold at DisneyQuest in Florida.

Game screen story sketch by Ray Cadd and Tracey Carpenter

World of Color concept by Danilo Gonzalez

The World Is a Carousel of Color

One of the first major elements of the makeover of Disney California Adventure was the World of Color show that takes over Paradise Bay every night and gives the Park a fitting finale to its day. Taking its theme and name from the classic Walt Disney television show, *Wonderful World of Color*, the show, which debuted in 2010, is a montage of many classic moments from Disney films over the years—both animated and live action. And just as *Wonderful World of Color* celebrated the newfound magic of *color* television, World of Color celebrates the technology we have today. During the presentation, water is filled with color via LED lighting, the projection of high-fidelity imagery, and many other technological tricks that we have at our disposal.

The show is held primarily on a massive show rig that rises up out of the water for showtime but recedes below the surface for the rest of the day. This platform is home to the many nozzles, lights, projectors, fountains, mist curtains, and flame and pyrotechnic systems that make the show such an incredible spectacle. Other elements from the surrounding locations in Paradise Pier are brought into play via additional lighting effects, lasers, and the placement of the audio system so that the whole land is brought to life.

QUICK TAKES

• The World of Color show platform is nearly 400 feet by 175 feet, or roughly the size of a football field.

• It features more than 1,000 nozzles and fountains, some of which are capable of shooting water 200 feet in the air.

• The advanced show control system allows for frequent updates, so that the show can remain fresh and surprising for our guests.

Great care is taken in establishing the transitions between sequences, so that one flows seamlessly into the next. Color and movement and even relationships between content and even subject matter in adjacent scenes are used to establish these connections. The end result is a compendium show that maintains its own internal thread of logic. These sequence concept sketches by Richard Improta illustrate the point.

Wall•E

The Roman goddess Diana fires an arrow into the sky to form the stars, after which the arrow actually morphs into the character Eve. She and Wall•E re-create the famous dancing-in-space scene from the film.

Pocahontas

The water found "just around the river bend" and the "Colors of the Wind" are key thematic show elements in our story, and the movement of the leaves spans the entire platform, or stage, for the show.

The Lion King

The movement of the water and the lighting is intended to capture the "mood" of the scene rather than just serve as a projection backdrop for a movie. Instead, this movement is presented as an abstract expression of the scene.

Alice in Wonderland

This film is known for having one of the more vibrant color palettes ever put on-screen. In this unrealized concept, the ability to turn off fountains and make things seem to "disappear" worked very well for a character like the Cheshire Cat.

PACIFIC WHARF

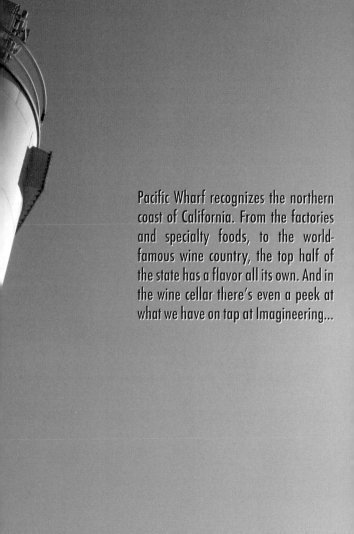

Pacific Wharf recognizes the northern coast of California. From the factories and specialty foods, to the world-famous wine country, the top half of the state has a flavor all its own. And in the wine cellar there's even a peek at what we have on tap at Imagineering...

Down on the Docks

Pacific Wharf overall concept by Ned Mueller

Pacific Wharf is an ode to the northern California coast, especially the Cannery Row area of Monterey near San Francisco. This part of Disney California Adventure is a romantic image of a waterfront industrial neighborhood, populated with all facets of the famed American "Melting Pot," each bringing its own identity and culture, and helping to make Pacific Wharf greater than the sum of its parts. This sense of community is a theme that runs throughout California's history, and that echoes the theme of our nation as a whole. Places like these are where people live and work and stitch together the fabric of communities.

The architecture of the land is that of an aged industrial district—with most buildings reflecting the early- to mid-twentieth century—with corrugated metal walls and roofs mingling with simple lap-sided carpentry. The land was character-finished by our paint and plaster teams to show its age and the patina that occurs over time. Pacific Wharf is an idealized vision of an industrial neighborhood, a celebration of the labors performed and the people who perform them.

Walt Disney once said, "You can design and create, and build the most wonderful place in the world. But it takes people to make the dream a reality." Places like Pacific Wharf, where people live and work, are not the ones that get the most attention, but they're the glue that holds a community together. For this reason, it's the part of the Park where we've chosen to place our preview center to tell you about the work that we're doing to bring more stories to our Parks.

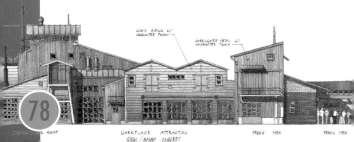

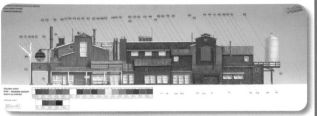

Color elevation by Sarah Mitchell, Anita Williams, and Crystal Speck

A Working Design

Even a design for a "working space" requires a lot of work! Our designers begin with real-world reference and research, and then put a great deal of thought into how to recombine the elements they find in that research to design a place that tells the story we want to tell. Even though we see industrial workplaces every day, we wanted Pacific Wharf to be evocative in a way that makes guests want to give it a second look, to dig deeper into understanding what this place is about. Our ideas of how to present this story evolved through many different design phases, with input from many disciplines along the way. Careful manipulation of forms, color, texture, surface detail, and character treatments make our compendium of real parts into something that you're not likely to find out in the real world.

Courtyard concept by Nina Rae Vaughn

Architectural elevation of Pacific Wharf facades by Coulter Winn

MARGARITA HUT   "WRITERS BAR"   BREWERY ENTRY

Wine casks display ideas being developed at WDI.

Just Around the Corner

Every fan of the Disney Parks feels immense anticipation while waiting for an exciting new attraction, land, or Park to make its debut once it's been announced. It's exciting to imagine the possibilities, but at the same time it's nice to get a little information about what's to come. Carefully building that anticipation was a hallmark of the way Walt generated interest in his ventures at Disneyland via his weekly television show. During the show, Walt would walk through the studios at Imagineering giving little glimpses of the work in progress that would lead to a great new addition to the Park.

As the remaking of Disney California Adventure approached, the Company sought to revive that tradition of building excitement and anticipation for the changes on the way. The Blue Sky Cellar was added as a preview center to highlight each wave of construction as it appeared on the horizon. Peeks at concept art, models on display, and video footage giving a behind-the-scenes look at the work that was happening told the story of the evolution of the Park. This feeding of our guests' curiosity continues at the Blue Sky Cellar even today, with ongoing previews of projects from all over the Disneyland Resort.

Preview graphic map of Cars Land by William Martinez

Bakery Tour activity concept by Ray Spencer

What's Cookin'?

The Bakery Tour is an example of how you can follow a particular thread of thought from one iteration to another within our work over the course of time. It is a remnant of an idea that at one point led to the development of The Disney Institute in Walt Disney World in Florida. Then-CEO Michael Eisner got excited about the idea of representing for guests the various ways in which people work in fields that may be different from their own. In the case of the Institute, this concept actually took the form of hands-on activities and classes that allowed visitors to try out a new form of work or an art or a craft in a very nurturing environment. Here at Pacific Wharf, the original idea was directed more toward giving guests a glimpse into the work the people of the state of California pursue. The Bakery Tour is a celebration of their labors and the areas in which they, in some cases, truly lead the way.

Bakery Tour building concept by Victor Post

Environmental graphics on the Pacific Wharf facade

Shout It from the Rooftops...and the Walls

In creating Park environments based on real places, environmental graphics are always a big part of the story. They are a part of the visual landscape, and their absence is very noticeable if they are not factored into our designs. Particularly in early industrial spaces, there is a very distinctive vocabulary of advertising and identification signage that makes re-creations of those spaces read as correct and believable. As the industrial architecture of America was formed, companies made their presence known through large, rooftop signage that could be seen from a distance, and large signs painted on walls that could be seen by nearby pedestrians or motorists. These graphics were embedded into the urban landscape. The practice continues today, with materials and methods of construction and design styles changing with the times. There is even a subcategory we refer to as "ghost graphics," which are remnants left behind by a prior tenant or activity. These are key scenic devices for us when creating urban spaces that are intended to have a visible history behind them.

QUICK TAKES

• For reasons related to back-of-house infrastructure, two restaurants in Pacific Wharf—Cocina Cucamonga and Lucky Fortune Cookery—actually switched places in 2009.

• The area including Wine Country Trattoria and the Walt Disney Imagineering Blue Sky Cellar is based on California's Wine Country, a renowned wine-producing region north of San Francisco. This part of the land serves as a transition from the forests of Grizzly Peak to the more urban waterfront locales.

Line Work

Pier poles, masts, and rigging for yardarms and cargo cranes are used by designers to create the identity of a dockside environment, like the one found at

Pacific Wharf. But they serve an additional function as well. Vertical and diagonal lines created by scenic elements such as these allow for dynamic compositions to be framed from multiple angles. Just as an art director would work on a film planned to be viewed on-screen, our teams work to ensure that any point of view found by the guests and their "walking cameras" will appeal to the eye.

We're on a Mission

California is known for its Mission Style architecture, which was brought to the region by Spanish missionaries who came to the New World to spread their faith. They built a series of structures up and down the coast, using them as churches and gathering places. With their wood framing, hand-formed plaster walls, and terra-cotta barrel-tile roofs, many of these Mission Style structures still remain throughout the state to this day and have become a distinctive part of California's architectural heritage. Many buildings constructed since those early examples have taken their lead from this clearly recognizable style. It also influenced some aspects of the California Craftsman style.

The Wine Country Trattoria and the adjacent Walt Disney Imagineering Blue Sky Cellar feature the Spanish Mission Style so prevalent in Sonoma Valley and the wine regions of Northern California.

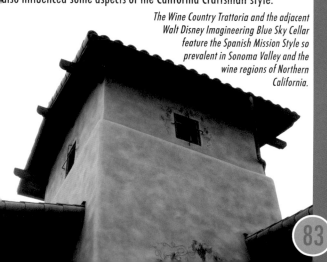

Concept for the dining courtyard at Boardwalk Pizza & Pasta by Christopher Smith

The Whole Story

A guest's memory of a day at a Disney Park is a summation of a great many experiences. Much of that comes from time spent with the friends and family with whom they came to the Park. Clearly their immersion into the world of the Park itself and its many varied attractions are a huge part of that, but there's much more. The addition of complementary offerings—in the form of dining and shopping locations that are coordinated with both the central and individual stories of the Park—goes a long way toward rounding out the full measure of a day spent in these environments. The entertainment aspect of many of our dining options, as well as the ability to take home a souvenir commemorating the event, extends the world of the Park, adding richness, depth, and variety to the guests' experiences.

Our retail and food and beverage locations are designed to blend into and augment the stories of the Park. The architecture and set dressings are approached in just the same way as they would be on an attraction. The choices of what to serve or sell there are derived from the definition of the place and the ideas of who would "live" there. Imagineers work with the Company's fantastic chefs to brainstorm menu concepts to fit into each land, and we collaborate with our product planners to suggest key items that might be of value to our guests based on the experiences we are striving to create. The cumulative effect of all of this effort and coordination is a seamless environment in which no single element pulls you out of the story, and everything you see, do, and eat only adds to the effect.

Graphic design for Lucky Fortune Cookery in the Pacific Wharf area

LUCKY FORTUNE COOKERY

Pacific Rim Foods

Tasteful and Timely

Some food and beverage locations within our Parks create experiences unto themselves, such as the grand drinking and dining venues of the Carthay Circle Theatre. Those restaurants and lounges cast you in a role and put you in the shoes of a Hollywood sophisticate from the heyday back in Walt's time. In other instances the connection to the Park's story lines can be a simple bit of nomenclature or a design detail—for example, Taste Pilot's Grill, which references the aviators of Condor Flats and is dressed to look like an airplane maintenance hangar. Our Parks need to offer our guests a great variety of food types, so sometimes that bit of scenic overlay is as far as the story needs to be taken. A place like Corn Dog Castle or Clarabelle's Hand-Scooped Ice Cream can transport the guest back to another time via the enjoyment of simple pleasures like a well-made corn dog or a hand-dipped ice cream bar.

On the retail side, some locations are absolutely specific to a time and place and a story line—as is the case with the Tower Hotel Gifts shop at the exit of the The Twilight Zone Tower of Terror ™. That store is very much woven into the story of that attraction, and the merchandise available inside is connected very closely to the identity of the hotel that hosts this very popular ride. Other shops play a broader role in the placemaking of the lands within the Park. Elias & Co. on Buena Vista Street plays much the same role as The Emporium on Main Street, U.S.A. in Disneyland—serving as just the sort of department store that would have defined a commercial street in the turn-of-the-century, small-town Midwest or in 1920s-era Los Angeles. These stores also serve the very functional purpose of providing for our guests the broadest selection of merchandise, both core to the Park itself and some of the more popular specialty items from throughout the Park.

Interior concept for Elias & Co. by Victor Post and William Martinez

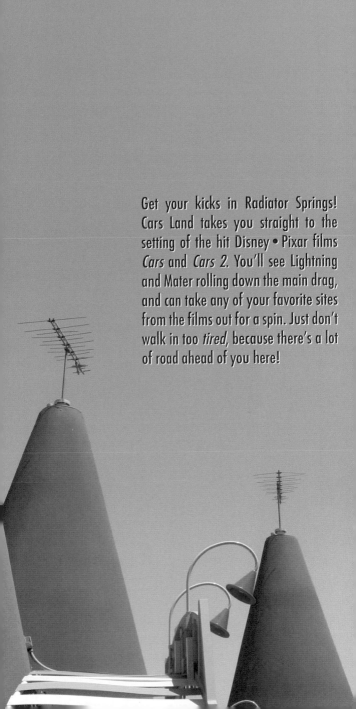

Get your kicks in Radiator Springs! Cars Land takes you straight to the setting of the hit Disney•Pixar films *Cars* and *Cars 2.* You'll see Lightning and Mater rolling down the main drag, and can take any of your favorite sites from the films out for a spin. Just don't walk in too *tired,* because there's a lot of road ahead of you here!

Setting the Scene

Cars Land aerial illustration by Dan Goozeé

Driving for the Finish Line

Rolling off the assembly line in the summer of 2012, Cars Land—the largest addition ever built at Disney California Adventure—arose from a former backstage parking lot that had been designated for Park expansion. This new and original land was presented as the culmination of the multiyear makeover of the Park, and was its crowning achievement. It is one of the most detailed, elaborate, and complete environments that Imagineering has ever created.

The land and the characters, attractions, and experiences found within are inspired by the 2006 Disney•Pixar film *Cars*, and its 2011 sequel, *Cars 2*. The story of a remote stop on the legendary Route 66 connects to the well-known California car culture. The rich tapestry of these long-forgotten locales combined with the body of knowledge of a good many car nuts on both the Pixar and WDI teams result in an amazing collection of experiences that truly allow our guests to step into Radiator Springs and take in a car's-eye view. What guests find in Cars Land is a painstaking re-creation of many of the places and elements that made the town in the film so evocative—only here they're free to decide for themselves where the road ahead will take them!

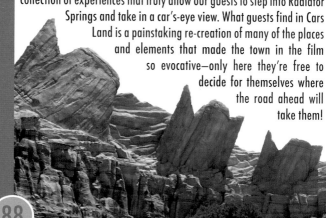

10-4, Good Buddies!

Cars Land represents one of the earliest fruits of the 2006 acquisition by The Walt Disney Company of Pixar Animation Studios, and the largest collaboration to date between the Imagineers and the animators from Pixar. The concept went into development in earnest not long after the combination of the two companies, and the two groups were joined at the fender for the duration of the project. From concept to production and field art direction, the creators of the films worked hand in hand with the creators of the land.

Cars Land logo, developed by Pixar Animation Studios

UICK TAKES

• Imagineers used digital models of Radiator Springs created at Pixar during the making of the film *Cars* in order to plan and even build elements of the land.

• The larger features of the amazing rockwork vista that frames Cars Land were placed to screen particular visual intrusions from the city of Anaheim outside the Park boundary.

• The Imagineering core team retraced many of the same steps taken by the original film team in their research trip on Route 66.

Luigi's Flying Tires paint elevation by Trung Ngo

Radiator Springs scene by Chris Turner

Ka-Chow!!!

Some films seem as though they were made to become Disney Park attractions, and *Cars* was certainly one of them. The tremendous success of the film, as well as the following that developed for the toys and other products based on these characters and the world they inhabit, made it clear that guests would leap at the opportunity to get behind the wheel and go for a spin—and even a race—through the world of Route 66 and the desert Southwest. So we get to go for that ride in one of the largest and most technologically sophisticated attractions we've ever built.

Radiator Springs Racers features an extravaganza of multimedia storytelling devices compiled to deliver on the scope and scale one would expect from a ride based on this source material. The massive rockwork facade and wide-open expanses serve as our backdrop for significant portions of the ride. When we enter the show building, we encounter large-format Audio-Animatronics characters moving around in traditional show scenes, and combinations of real elements and effects that seamlessly transport us to the "Mother Road" and back.

Many of our graphic designs, like this marquee for Radiator Springs Racers, serve both show and functional purposes. They have to help tell our stories, assist our guests in navigating the Park, and inform them of how to use various entrances to the attraction.

Every Trick in the Trunk

Nothing we do is "standardized" from attraction to attraction, or even from character to character within a given show. On Radiator Springs Racers, our character development and animation teams were confronted with several unique challenges. Just as the Pixar animation team had to develop new techniques to bring their vision for each character to the screen, the Imagineers on this project had to try out new ways of bringing them to life. Each of the cars in the film presented its own set of design characteristics and, therefore, was approached in a different way in order to create the Audio-Animatronics version.

First comes a detailed study of each character—its physical characteristics, its behavior, all of the things that make it who it is. Talking cars are not like anything we had ever built before, so none of our prior approaches applied. The cars in the film are made of metal and glass and plastic. Our versions of them need to appear to be mechanical, while also having very fluid, organic, anthropomorphic movement.

Some *Cars* characters, like Sheriff and Doc Hudson, have bumpers and other design elements that allowed us to create separations for movement in a way that was more or less like that of human and other characters that we have built. On the cars, however, those pieces were of a scale and required a flexibility that we had not attempted before. Lightning McQueen, on the other hand, is a race car. He doesn't have visible bumpers or other mechanical elements with which to form mouth movements. He has smooth surfaces and very organic movement when he speaks. This led to the development of internal rear-projection techniques to enable his mouth animation. The blending of the projected surfaces into the real ones is the real trick there.

Early conceptual bird's-eye by Jim Shull

A Sketchy Process

One of the remarkable legacies of Walt's early animation Studio was the introduction of the storyboarding process, in which the key story points in a film—or a Disney Park attraction—are lined up sequentially so that the team can verify that the story they hope to tell is coming through in the way it is intended. This is done early in the process before production, so that we focus our energies where appropriate.

Storyboards are typically drawn very quickly and are sometimes painted or colored, sometimes not. They focus on the action in the story—the delivery of dialogue, the major events as seen from the point of view of the guest, and the results of these story beats. The team reviews the storyboards, uses them as a backdrop for verbal presentations, and maintains them as a working story puzzle that is continually updated as new ideas come up. The process tends to precede the heavy development work on a show, but continues throughout.

A Means to "The End"

Storyboards are by no means considered to be a finished design effort. The elements are shown in rough form and require a great deal of further development. Their very purpose dictates that they are in a way "expendable." Of course that doesn't mean that they are not incredibly valuable, but that their value is derived from the fact that they can be changed or dropped as necessary as the project is developed.

So, story points that aren't working during reviews or that can be improved upon are left behind. The Radiator Springs Racers storyboards by Chris Turner seen on these pages demonstrate that, as some of these examples did not make it into the finished attraction. Edits and deletions can happen for many different reasons, from staging or logistical challenges to pure storytelling. The team cannot hold storyboard sketches to be too precious, because if they aren't working within the flow of the show, they have to be cut.

Luigi's Flying Tires

Luigi's Flying Tires concept by Mike Overman

Flying, Again...

Luigi's Flying Tires is an attraction with a very strong Disneyland connection. It represents a revival of an idea that Imagineering was forced to abandon in 1966. We went back to it as soon as the opportunity presented itself to update and improve upon it, because it was a good idea and we never truly let those go. The Flying Saucers in Tomorrowland began flying in 1961 but only lasted for about six years due to concerns revolving around capacity and the fact that they were difficult to maintain. But many members of the Cars Land team remembered them very fondly and jumped at the opportunity to bring them back to our guests in a new guise and with newfound solutions to the issues that plagued the original.

As the engineering challenges were addressed, attention turned toward expanding the experience beyond the ride itself and into the world of *Cars*. The charming characters Luigi and Guido become the stars, with their personalities and their intense affinity for auto racing demonstrated through the lovingly displayed *car*tifacts of their favorite racers and races. The propping and graphics found throughout their meticulously kept garage tell us so much about them and their fandom.

Notated concept elevation for Luigi's queue by Wesley Keil

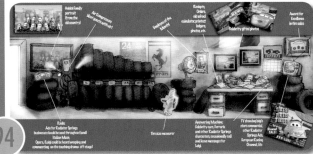

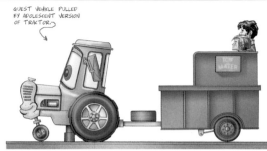

GUEST VEHICLE PULLED BY ADOLESCENT VERSION OF TRACTOR.

TOW MATER'S JUNKYARD JAMBOREE
CARSLAND · DCA · JIM SHULL · 9·07

Junkyard Jamboree ride vehicle elevation by Jim Shull

Doh-See-Tow!

For Mater's Junkyard Jamboree, a fun and clever little spinning ride, the focus was on the musical accompaniment. Often the music or songs that serve as the soundtracks for our attractions are the most memorable part. The songs get stuck in your head and become a part of how our guests share their recollections of their Disney Park experiences.

Blaring from Mater's junkyard jukebox, these seven original songs were all written for the attraction and recorded by Larry the Cable Guy, the voice of Mater from the Cars films. Listen closely, and you might just hear Mater forget a few lyrics every once in a while.

QUICK TAKES

• The songs were written by Bruno Coons, composer for the Cars Toons shorts, and include one song that was cowritten by Mr. Coons and Imagineering Show Writer Kevin Rafferty.

• Two songs written for the ride, "Welcome to Radiator Springs" and "Radiator Rock," were adapted for the land's background music.

Mater's Junkyard Jamboree bird's-eye illustration by Mike Overman

Ornament Valley color keys by Bill Cone

A Different Perspective

Imagineers play with scale in different ways in order to make elements in the Park look larger or smaller or even farther away than they are in reality. But there are other ways to trick the eye. Color, too, can come into play to imply distance. As objects get farther and farther away from us, they also tend to become less saturated in color and have less contrast between the highlights and shadows. This is known as atmospheric perspective—an effect that has been put to great use over the years in painting and is evident when you look closely at landscape photography.

Our Ornament Valley is intended to represent a vast swath of the American Southwest, suggesting vistas far greater than we could ever actually build here within the footprint of this Park. So our character paint team dealt with each successive "plane" of canyon wall with progressively softer and less chromatic hues and values. In setting the direction for the character painting on the rockwork facades, the team turned first to artists at Pixar who had created the original color styling during the development of *Cars*. The pastel color keys they produced evoke the setting while also employing atmospheric perspective to imply the distance we needed to suggest. Even when standing right in front of our fabricated range, your eye is fooled into believing that the farthest ridges are significantly farther away than they really are.

Capping It All Off

Every little element is up for being rethought. Here we see a radiator cap used as a finial on the top of a stanchion post in the queue for Mater's Junkyard Jamboree. Pay attention as you make your way through the land. You never know what you'll find around these *parts*.

In addition to the play on words in the name applied to each of Mater's "cow" tractors, each one carries its own unique spot and rust pattern, as no two cows ever truly look alike!

Many details found in Mater's Junkyard relate to the expanded world of *Cars*, including the popular Cars Toons short films. In these, Mater takes on the persona of a firefighter, a bullfighter, a doctor, and stunt truck extraordinaire Mater the Greater.

Get your graphics on Route 66.

Signature Signs

One of the recognizable features of the world of Route 66 is its amazing signage. The fun and showmanship mixed with the amazing patina demonstrating the considerable mileage accrued create an unmistakable look. Our show writers have worked with our graphic designers to place environmental graphics throughout the land. Some offer funny plays on words, and some just further the placemaking effort.

97

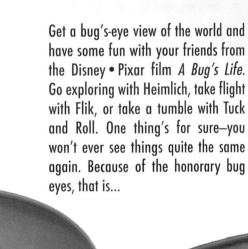

Get a bug's-eye view of the world and have some fun with your friends from the Disney•Pixar film *A Bug's Life*. Go exploring with Heimlich, take flight with Flik, or take a tumble with Tuck and Roll. One thing's for sure—you won't ever see things quite the same again. Because of the honorary bug eyes, that is...

Concept illustration of land entry by Christopher Smith

Part-Time Design

When an animation studio sets out to make a film such as *A Bug's Life*, they are telling a story in the highly visual medium of motion pictures. The design of the film as it appears on-screen is an integral part of the storytelling in this medium. As characters are developed in concert with the world in which the story takes place, the work of the designers and art directors on the film expands upon the script, and every design choice is made with the intent to further the telling of the story.

The environment or set design tells us about the nature of the place in which the events take place, which provides context for the story. The prop design tells us about the personality traits of the characters through the details with which they surround themselves. Costume design further fleshes out the characters and the ways in which they see themselves or others see them. Once the "rules" are established by the story, the director, and the design team, the exercise of fleshing out the design becomes a parallel to the architectural idea of kit-of-parts.

In kit-of-parts design, a defined set of elements—which can be configured in multiple ways to achieve the intent—is available to the designer. The logic of a kit-of-parts is applicable to the world of the bugs in the film and in our land, because the "kit" is defined by the elements that would be available to the characters in order to build the world in which they live. In the case of *A Bug's Life*, the environment is comprised only of things that are within the reach of the bugs, either found in their natural environment or left behind by humans.

The resourcefulness and inventiveness of the bugs is expressed through the playful arrangement and modification of objects from the designers' kit-of-parts. Visual humor is created through the distortion of scale between the human world and the bug world. It makes this film and land unlike any other.

Bug-Brain Design

In creating "A Bug's Land," the design exercise for the Imagineers was to put themselves into the mind-set of the bugs and to look at the world from their point of view. From a repurposed tissue box standing in for a restroom to a firefly hanging from a flexible drinking straw serving as a streetlamp, the kit-of-parts for "A Bug's Land" creates a steady stream of visual gags and contextual humor. The land is populated with clever inventions cobbled together by the bugs out of twigs, leaves, and rocks, and found objects that are given new life and new purpose in ways evident only to the bugs. They are resourceful and have created a world for themselves with almost all of our modern conveniences! Inspired by Flik, who is always looking for ways to improve life for all bugkind, the Imagineers had to think like a bug to design this land.

Flik's Flyers vehicle concept sketch by Steve Beyer

QUICK TAKES

• "A Bug's Land" was the first major expansion of Disney California Adventure. Work was begun almost immediately upon the opening of the Park, and the new land debuted in late 2002.

• "A Bug's Land" replaced and expanded upon the former Bountiful Valley Farm section of the Park. Only It's Tough to be a Bug! remains from that predecessor.

Overview of "A Bug's Land" by Christopher Smith

Early concept for entry to It's Tough to be a Bug! by Ray Spencer

Working Out the Bugs

The anchor attraction of "A Bug's Land"—It's Tough to be a Bug!—first appeared at Disney's Animal Kingdom in 1998, housed within that Park's icon, the Tree of Life. That version of the attraction actually debuted before the theatrical release of *A Bug's Life*. After the second iteration opened with Disney California Adventure in 2001, it remained in place as "A Bug's Land" was built around it in 2002.

This theatrical experience involves more than just the film on-screen. It begins with the image rendered in three dimensions via polarized lenses, 90 degrees opposed to one another, each visible from one of the viewer's two eyes. Additionally, there are Audio-Animatronics characters placed in the theater to bring the story to life around you. Lighting furthers the action from the film throughout the theater environment. Built-in special effects, such as liquid nitrogen fog systems, air cannons, water spritzers, a bee sting in the back, and rappelling spiders, all work together to surround and surprise the audience.

There are characters created solely for this show as well. Chili the tarantula, the Termitator, Claire de Room, the Heckler Bug, and many other, smaller bugs and butterflies make up the cast. Inspired by those in the film, these additional characters were designed and developed to flesh out this world in a way that is consistent, and to allow us to create an original story that extends that of the film for our Park experience.

Heckler Bug color studies by Doug Griffith

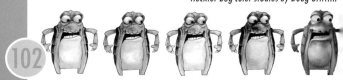

DisneyVision!

It's Tough to be a Bug! is part of a continuum of multimedia theatrical presentations that trace a Disney lineage dating all the way back to "A Tour of the West" in Disneyland in 1955. Beginning with the earliest Circarama (later, Circle-Vision) films that enveloped the audience in a 360-degree field of view, Walt and his Imagineers have looked for ways to make motion pictures that were more immersive and even multisensory. Employing 3-D capabilities, scents, in-theater effects, and even Audio-Animatronics and performers, these films are able to envelope our guests as they become caught up in the world in which the story takes place. The following attractions, listed here by the order in which they first appeared, represent the progression of these films.

A Tour of the West, Disneyland, 1955

Magic Journeys, Epcot, 1982

Captain EO, Epcot, 1986

Jim Henson's Muppet*Vision 3D, Disney's Hollywood Studios, 1991

Visionarium, Disneyland Paris, 1992

Honey, I Shrunk the Audience, Epcot, 1994

It's Tough to be a Bug!, Disney's Animal Kingdom, 1998

CinéMagique, Walt Disney Studios Paris, 2002

Mickey's PhilharMagic, Magic Kingdom, 2003

QUICK TAKES

• The character Hopper represents one of our most complicated Audio-Animatronics figures ever. He has seventy functions—or points of movement—that control his various actions; it's an Imagineering record!

• Andrew Stanton—the codirector and cowriter of *A Bug's Life*—performed the voice of Hopper for It's Tough to be a Bug!

• The Disney California Adventure version of It's Tough to be a Bug! brings with it the thematic environmental message embedded in the show for its role at Disney's Animal Kingdom. The show demonstrates the need for us to recognize the value of the bugs with whom we share the planet, and tells us to appreciate them!

103

Area development and leaf color studies by Richard Broderick

Leaf Nothing to Chance

At the outset of the development of *A Bug's Life*, the animators at Pixar did camera tests in which they placed small cameras very low to the ground to get a sense of what a bug's-eye view of the world would be. One of their key discoveries was that when looking up through the plants in the direction of the sunlight, they appear to be translucent. There was much

more softness and tonal variety in the coloration of the leaves than the filmmakers had anticipated. In fact, much of the internal vein structure of the plant was often visible through the leaf surface. This led to some technical challenges that had to be factored into the environmental design of the artists' digital world, but meeting those challenges was key to the believability as well as the beauty of the film.

In creating "A Bug's Land," our technical challenge was to find a way to build giant clover stalks using materials that would give the translucent look that we needed in order to match the film, but also provide the rain and sun protection that we desired, hold up to architectural standards, and meet our expectations on durability. In this case, the answer was a nylon-reinforced vinyl material, stretched over a steel frame and colored with a very carefully balanced color gradation that would offer that shift in opacity toward the open areas of the leaves. So the effect one sees when walking beneath them is that of dappled light hitting the ground, and glimpses of sunlight when one looks up. Luckily, you can even find one four-leaf clover in the land!

Prize Inside

All of the architectural elements in "A Bug's Land" are derived from human leftovers—various boxes and umbrellas—including this entry corridor that takes us into the land. In order to detail these elements so that they are identifiable as the intended source material, our writers and designers work together to develop content with which to cover the surfaces. Often the result, such as the hidden prize "printed" inside this cereal box, becomes as much entertainment as environment.

I See the Light

Where would nighttime light come from in a bug's world? They don't have any means of generating electricity, after all. From a firefly, of course! These cute little guys use their natural talents—as well as a resourcefully assembled light-directing cone—to help us find our way when the sun goes down.

Bug Built

Even simple graphics like a restroom sign get the kit-of-parts treatment. A mixture of man-made and natural elements, this sign was presumably assembled by a graphic designer bug who looked at what he or she had available and came up with the best way possible to identify the facilities. The information has to be clearly legible but is rendered as though by a bug's...hand?

Flik's Flyers concept illustration by Steve Beyer

Following the Rules

In Flik's Flyers, the kit-of-parts approach is taken to something of an extreme in terms of the variety of parts brought to bear. Imagineering great Marc Davis stated that when you set out to create the worlds that we create in these storytelling environments—in his case referring to both animated films and Disney Parks—you can make the rules whatever you want them to be, but that once you have set those rules you need to hold yourself to them as your design progresses. You must adhere to the internal logic of the design and the story in order to maintain the believability of it. Sometimes this need for story continuity affects our design approach on a given attraction.

For example, it would not have been believable, within the rules of this world that has been created, for each of the gondolas and balloons to be identical. They are supposed to have been constructed by Flik out of found objects and materials, both natural and man-made, so the designers had to come up with eight different designs for the "boxes" Flik used to build this contraption, and eight different color schemes for the leaves.

Vehicle paint elevation by Ray Spencer and Jacqueline Spears

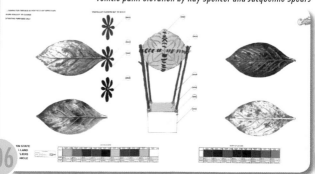

The Real Jitterbug

Vehicle design sketch by Larry Nikolai

A new spin on our old standard, Mad Tea Party, Francis' Ladybug Boogie gives "A Bug's Land" a whirling dervish of a twirling ride. As Francis teaches you how to dance, you know who's leading—you're just along for the ride! In an attraction such as this one, the challenge for the Imagineer is in finding the appropriate visual pun or repurposing of an element from the scaled-up human world that the bugs inhabit.

The design of the ride vehicles themselves is key to defining the experience visually. Developed just the way an animator would approach a drawing for a frame of film on-screen, Francis's face—gracing the front of each *buggy*—captures the essence of his distinctive personality in one key pose. The designer worked over a base drawing of the mechanical requirements of the carriage—built around the ergonomics of the guests who will be riding in it—and overlays a new drawing that fleshes out the creative intent while maintaining all of the necessary clearances and working within the capabilities of the materials with which it will be manufactured.

Concept for Francis' Ladybug Boogie by Steve Beyer

Concept for Heimlich's Chew Chew Train by Steve Beyer

A Bite-Size Attraction

Every movie has a character who steals—or eats—the show, as the case may be. In the case of *A Bug's Life*, that character was Heimlich, the happy caterpillar who longs to become a "beautiful butterfly!" In part due to his charming character design, but mostly owing to the hilarious vocal performance by Joe Ranft—the noted Pixar story lead who voiced several beloved characters for the Studio—Heimlich's was the breakout performance upon the release of the film. He has a similar effect on this attraction in our Park, as he narrates our train ride through the oversize (or is it bug-size?) backyard as only Heimlich could. His German-accented observations tend toward the nonsensical and the food-obsessed. When you're Heimlich, *everything* looks like a tasty bite!

Paint elevations for Heimlich's Chew Chew Train ride vehicle Larry Nikolai, and show set watermelon by Laurie New

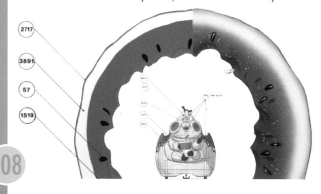

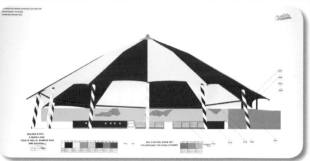

Tuck and Roll's Drive 'Em Buggies paint elevation by Michael Bishop

Under the Big Top

The design of Tuck and Roll's Drive 'Em Buggies is all about fun. In the same manner that Tuck and Roll stole their scenes in *A Bug's Life*, the Imagineers on this project team threw themselves with reckless abandon into the task of making this attraction into good, silly fun. From the playful design of the vehicles, which put the guest into the roles of Tuck and Roll themselves, to the straws for support columns and the Christmas tree lights as festoons, every bit of visual punnery is there to enhance the act. Guests hurl themselves at one another just like the two acrobatic bugs during their circus act. Our kit-of-parts from the movie in this case provided us with the idea for the building itself—while the canopy for Tuck and Roll's Drive 'Em Buggies is based on the circus tent umbrella that appeared in the film.

Tuck and Roll's Drive 'Em Buggies concept by Steve Beyer

HOLLYWOOD LAND

Head to Hollywood Land to see why so many people have been drawn to the movie business. From Walt's time to today, Hollywood has been the stuff of dreams—a town filled with movie magic where stars are made. Take in a Disney show at the Hyperion Theater and get a glimpse of how Disney Animation is brought to life. Just make sure you're ready for your close-up!

Hollywood street scene by Greg Wilzbach

And We're...Rolling!

Make no mistake—Hollywood is *the* reason Walt came to California. He knew there was no better place for him to pursue the medium of animation than in the hotbed of American filmmaking. The artists, the studios, the distributors, and all of the components of the fledgling motion picture industry were all there for him to tap into. So Hollywood is a key element of the Disney story and of the entirety of Disney California Adventure. In a way, Hollywood serves as the underpinning of the rest of the Park as well, showing us all of the varied aspects of the state of California as viewed through a Hollywood lens.

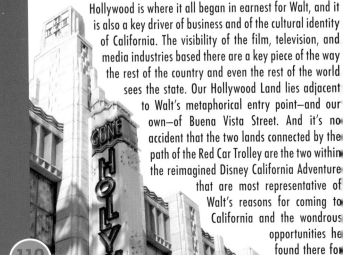

Hollywood is where it all began in earnest for Walt, and it is also a key driver of business and of the cultural identity of California. The visibility of the film, television, and media industries based there are a key piece of the way the rest of the country and even the rest of the world sees the state. Our Hollywood Land lies adjacent to Walt's metaphorical entry point—and our own—of Buena Vista Street. And it's no accident that the two lands connected by the path of the Red Car Trolley are the two within the reimagined Disney California Adventure that are most representative of Walt's reasons for coming to California and the wondrous opportunities he found there for the taking.

A Trolley Runs Through It

Besides the obvious placemaking benefits of the Red Car Trolley, this key feature adds an important kinetic element to the streetscape. Its movement activates the environment and augments the spatial relationships in the architecture. It helps bring this faux environment

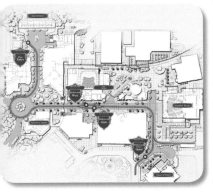

to life while further reinforcing our time and place setting. Seeing the Red Car running up and down the street implicitly sends the message that this isn't the California of today.

Map of the Red Car Trolley route through Buena Vista Street and Hollywood Land

This color elevation of the Red Car Trolley was one of several distinct color studies that was selected as the final look of the train car. It features the iconic red with orange and white accents.

QUICK TAKE

• Prior to the redevelopment of Disney California Adventure, this land—known at the time as Hollywood Pictures Backlot—focused more on modern-day Hollywood. While there were elements that represented vintage buildings, the focus of the signage and the stories was less about that history. Drawing on Hollywood's past was a key focus of the redevelopment work.

Street level POV sketch by Greg Wilzbach

Disney Animation

The Magic of Disney Animation exterior by Jerry Bingham

Animation Fixation

If the heart of The Walt Disney Company is the Studio, then the heart of the Studio is Walt Disney Animation Studios. This really is where it all began, and where we still derive most of our inspiration. Walt drove his animators to constantly push the boundaries of the form and essentially redefine the technique, which led to Walt's name eventually becoming nearly synonymous with animation itself. Over the years, the Studio grew and changed locations, but animation has always remained central to what Disney does.

In order to tell the story of Disney in Hollywood, we have to tell the story of animation. At the Disney Animation attraction, it's about the process, the history, and the mind-set that drives the people who create animation—and even some tips and tricks to help a budding animator get started down that path. There are many experiences to explore here that offer inspiration, or at least foster an even greater appreciation for the art form.

The large crossroads space in the center of the attraction serves as a hub of sorts for moving from show to show within the overall Disney Animation pavilion. This space delivers an entrancing media presentation involving still images and video showing many favorite pieces of animation as they made their way through the process from sketch to screen. A versatile show, it presents enough of a show to enjoy while perhaps taking a respite before heading into the ancillary spaces; but for people who are really just passing through on their way to see the rest of the offerings, it creates a strong visual link to the subject matter.

Deeper Dive

The Animation Academy gives guests a chance to try their own hand at drawing a character under the tutelage of one of our instructors. Through these sessions, guests gain insight into the things an animator has to think about while "acting" out scenes on paper. This sort of participatory activity increases their appreciation of the efforts of the Disney animators.

Turtle Talk with Crush allows guests to carry on a conversation with Crush from *Finding Nemo* via a real-time animation system. Crush asks a lot of questions and tries his fin at figuring out the human world via these interactions. This attraction gives a peek into the principles of character development, and makes clear the fact that Crush truly does see the world—or at least the underwater portion of it—very differently than we do. An animator has to put him or herself inside the mind of the character in order to bring it to life.

In the Sorcerers Workshop, a series of experiences allows guests to delve into the particular personality quirks, traits, and histories of many of the Disney characters. This is a type of show element that relies heavily on our show writers to determine the best way to present information and to pull the guest into this exploration in a meaningful way. It's not just about the voice-over or the copy that shows up on the screen, but about the structure and the nature of the questions and the logic behind it all.

Sorcerers Workshop concept by Chip Pace

The Hollywood Land area restroom block building

The Wright Way to Design a Restroom

No part of the show receives short shrift when it comes to the Imagineering treatment. Even a purely functional—and very necessary—item such as a restroom building is subject to a design pass in order to make it fit into the Park and even, in this case, to further our placemaking efforts. The area restroom in Hollywood Land is designed to evoke the architecture of Frank Lloyd Wright—specifically his "textile block" or patterned concrete, style of building, which Wright employed in designing many well-known buildings in Southern California. These include Ennis House in Los Feliz (a neighborhood in Los Angeles), Millard House in Pasadena, and the Storer and Freeman houses in Hollywood.

It's the Little Things That Make All the Difference

The differences between the modern built environment and the times and places we tend to reference in our Parks often revolve around the absence or presence of intricate details and the ornate architectural ornamentation of earlier eras. As the cost of labor has risen and the majority of building came to be done with efficiency as the paramount priority, we have lost much of this handcrafted detail. It's one of the things that makes the Parks so inviting and helps us to take our guests away from the world they are used to.

Check out this advertisement to see these teaser images of all the sights to see in Disney California Adventure.

A Sign o' the Times

One of the signs seen on the side of the Magic of Disney Animation building opposite the Hyperion Theater is this familiar-looking sign identifying the "Walt Disney Studios." This version is made to recall the design of the famed marquee that sat atop Walt's original animation studio on Hyperion Avenue near Hollywood. The references to Mickey Mouse and Silly Symphonies clue you in as to the time period. Walt and Roy's enterprise made its home on Hyperion Avenue from 1925 to 1940.

WALT DISNEY STUDIOS
MICKEY MOUSE
AND
SILLY SYMPHONY
SOUND CARTOONS

A Peek Behind the Curtain

When we make our way around the corners into the Hollywood Studios Backlot area of Hollywood Land, we get glimpses of the armature holding these pieces of scenery in place. This is a subtle reminder of the sleight of hand—so common in the world of Hollywood—that makes you believe you're in a different place. The movie business is based on this ability to transport an audience, and Imagineering's origins in the Disney film Studio make this part of our legacy as well.

117

The Twilight Zone Tower of Terror™

A conceptual image can be used to illustrate more than just the details of design, scale, and architecture that will define the physical appearance of the finished shows or attraction. As in this very atmospheric bird's-eye conceptual image by Victor Post, a beautiful rendering can also reveal the emotional intent of the experience that we are trying to create for our guests. The occlusion of portions of the building in the foggy night sky detracts from the specifics of the facade, but certainly adds to the mood of trepidation our guests will feel upon seeing this building.

Please Drop in for a Visit

One of the most striking attractions in all of the Disney Parks initially took up residence at the end of Sunset Boulevard in Disney's Hollywood Studios in 1994, and came to Disney California Adventure in 2004. The foreboding face of the Hollywood Tower Hotel serves as both a warning and a beacon to draw our guests through Hollywood Land. From the start, it's clear that something has gone wrong here. It's up to the guest to decide whether he or she is brave enough to go inside to find out what the trouble is. The attraction inside, The Twilight Zone Tower of Terror™, is one of the grandest examples of the art of the Disney themed show. Its mix of placemaking, storytelling, and thrills have made it a candidate for replication, so it can now also be found at Tokyo DisneySea and the Walt Disney Studios Paris. This one uses a Moorish Revival style as its design inspiration rather than the Spanish Colonial of the original.

In their search for a story backdrop that would be suitably scary—or at least creepy—for the experience they intended to create, the Imagineers looked outside the Disney universe and selected one of the best-known early television programs. *The Twilight Zone*® offers a ready-made world where nothing is as it appears and anything can happen and still make sense within the logic of the story.

What Goes Up Must Come Down…Quickly

The ride mechanism for The Twilight Zone Tower of Terror™ is as impressive as the attraction's imposing facade. Situated high above the rest of the Park atop the elevator shafts are a pair of electric motors capable of moving the ride vehicle through its 130-foot path of travel in no time flat. It reaches its top speed in less than 1.5 seconds, and the motors' massive torque provides a degree of control that offers the Imagineers the ability to decelerate the cab and move it in the opposite direction so smoothly that the riders sometimes don't know if they're going up or coming down. These massive motors are twelve feet tall, seven feet wide, thirty-five feet long, and had to be lifted into position with a crane—after which the building was completed around them, sealing the motors inside.

A Very Special Episode

Our story is set up by the inimitable Rod Serling, who appears in an introductory film in the library of the hotel. The clip was taken from an actual *Twilight Zone*® episode—"A Good Life"—and reappropriated with a very well-timed edit and a voice-over by a talented impersonator. This introductory film was directed by Joe Dante, who had directed a segment of the 1983 *Twilight Zone—The Movie*. Included among the sea of eye-catching props that give so much depth to the scenery are numerous references to characters or episodes from the classic television series.

Your elevator cab awaits in this color elevation by Suzanne Rattigan.

BOILER ROOM ELEVATION   SCENE 5
TWILIGHT ZONE
TOWER OF TERROR – DCA   FOR CHARACTER AGE INTENT ONLY

Traveling Show

The Twilight Zone Tower of Terror™ is featured in a different land in each of the four Disney Parks around the world in which it appears. It is found in Sunset Boulevard in Disney's Hollywood Studios, Hollywood Land in Disney California Adventure, Production Courtyard in Walt Disney Studios Paris, and American Waterfront in Tokyo DisneySea. Among Disney attractions, only Haunted Mansion is found in so many distinct lands. It speaks to the strength and versatility of the core concept, that it can be adapted in so many ways.

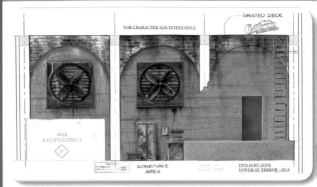

Boiler Room wall elevation by Suzanne Rattigan

Picture if You Will…

The Twilight Zone Tower of Terror™ required an amazing amount of development work, beginning with concept imagery and continuing all the way through to construction documents. The images on these pages will give you just a hint of some of the many avenues that have to be explored by our concept artists before a project can be fully formed for production. Each and every aspect from the long shot to the smallest details needs to be described visually before it can ever be turned into reality. Even in a case such as this, in which an earlier version of the attraction has been built elsewhere—at Disney's Hollywood Studios in Florida eight years earlier, as well as Disney Studios Paris and Tokyo DisneySea since—new work is done to distinguish each attraction from its siblings. This iteration of the attraction has a style all its own.

Concept elevation by Coulter Winn and Victor Post

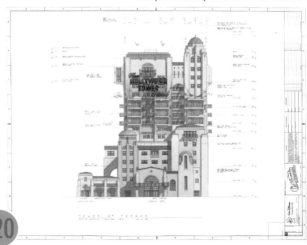

ARCH DETAIL CORRIDOR SCENE 7
TOWER OF TERROR

Color board for arch header by Suzanne Rattigan

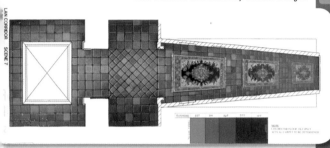

Color board for endless hallway floor by Suzanne Rattigan

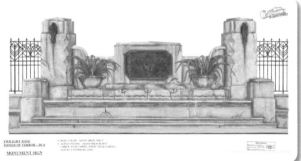

TWILIGHT ZONE
TOWER OF TERROR – DCA
MONUMENT SIGN

Paint elevation for entry fountain by Cindi Bothner
Electrical panel character concept by Cindi Bothner

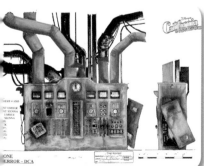

SCENE 5

TWILIGHT ZONE
TOWER OF TERROR – DCA

*Boiler character concept
by Suzanne Rattigan*

Monsters, Inc. Mike & Sulley to the Rescue!

Elevation of attraction facade by Larry Nikolai

The Attraction Under the Bed...

Bringing to life the world of the 2001 Disney•Pixar film, *Monsters, Inc.*, Monsters, Inc. Mike & Sulley to the Rescue! represents one of this Park's forays into the format of the classic Disneyland dark ride. Taking guests through favorite scenes from the film and allowing them to join in the chase to find Boo, it captures the spirit of the source material in the simple, charming way that has been the hallmark of Disney Parks since the opening of Disneyland in 1955. As the closest Park parallel to our animation Studio's well-known shorts, the dark ride relies on clear staging, easily understood visual storytelling, and the rapid pacing that ensures that a short maintains its energy from start to finish. The characters are posed and animated to deliver on their role. Throw in a few surprises along the way—like a color-changing Randall—and the effect is complete!

These lighting studies for scenes in the attraction by Chris Runco illustrate one of the parallels between the development processes for an Imagineering attraction versus an animated film. Many of the same tools used to focus the attention of film audiences are brought to bear to clearly communicate the story to our Park guests.

Character studies of Needleman and Smitty by Geefwee Boedoe

Go Figure

Before we can ever build an Audio-Animatronics character, a great deal of work has to go into developing the pose, the scale, the list of functions, and the mechanical infrastructure of that character. Each one is different, due to variations in size, relative proportions, and in the distinctive ways in which they move. Our artists work closely with our engineers to ensure that each group understands the needs of the other in order to present the finished show.

Sulley figure development sketches by Larry Nikolai

QUICK TAKES

• Monsters, Inc. Mike & Sulley to the Rescue! was the last Park attraction collaboration between Walt Disney Imagineering and Pixar Animation Studios before Pixar became part of The Walt Disney Company.

• Actual digital assets such as bulletin board material and product labels from the film production were used to dress scenes and to decorate propping in the attraction.

• Monsters, Inc. Mike & Sulley to the Rescue! took the place of the opening day attraction, Superstar Limo.

Storyboard sketches by Chris Turner and Laurie Newell

Disney Junior—Live on Stage!

The Streamline Moderne facade of Disney Junior—Live on Stage!

Making a Scene

One aspect of Hollywood that we wanted to bring to the Park is the world of television, and especially Disney's role in that. Disney Channel has been serving up entertainment for the whole family since 1983, and has found a particularly faithful audience for its Disney Junior block of children's programming. Disney Junior, in fact, is now even a sister network. Disney Junior—Live on Stage! brings those shows to life right before the eyes of our youngest guests. Seeing the familiar faces from their morning routine up onstage really brings kids into the worlds of these shows. It's an early introduction to theatrical conventions and to an understanding of the way shows can be translated for the stage.

This attraction is another example of a theatrical venue created by WDI with show content developed by Walt Disney Imagineering Creative Entertainment (WDI-CE). The format of Disney Junior—Live on Stage! allows for the content to be updated as new shows are brought into the rotation and become familiar to Park visitors. WDI-CE works with the Parks and with overall WDI leadership to determine the cycle for changes and updates to the show.

QUICK TAKE

• The venue began its existence as the Soap Opera Bistro, a restaurant celebrating the ongoing stories that viewers have become so attached to over the history of that genre.

• The previous show in this space was Playhouse Disney—Live on Stage!, based on a programming block on Disney Channel that was the precursor to Disney Junior.

Concept for Muppet*Vision 3D exterior by Tom Gilleon

Showtime!

Having first made its debut at Disney's Hollywood Studios in 1991, Muppet*Vision 3D was an opening day attraction bringing to this Park the zany world of the Muppets created by Jim Henson. At the time this attraction was developed and implemented, the Muppets were not yet a part of The Walt Disney Company, but they have since joined the fold in a 2004 purchase. Jim Henson's commitment to character development and maintaining an internal integrity to the stories being told was very much in alignment with Walt Disney's, and Muppet*Vision 3D was the last film project of Jim Henson's illustrious career in entertainment. The madcap backstage irreverence of the Muppets is a perfect vehicle to wreak havoc with the notion of a stage show. Between the well-intentioned mishaps and the curmudgeonly commentary offered up by the peanut gallery of the famed Waldorf and Stadler, this show is fun from start to finish.

Muppet*Vision 3D is a great example of the ways WDI often combines technologies in order to tell our stories. This is truly a multimedia presentation, employing almost all the tricks we have up our sleeves to envelope the audience in the environment and all of the events taking place around them. There is the film—a 3-D presentation that gives depth to the screen and brings the action to us. There are Audio-Animatronics figures in front of the stage and in surprising locations in the opera boxes and even behind the audience. There are special effects, both on-screen and in the theater. Bubbles and water droplets rain down on the audience from above. Fog effects drive home the cannon blasts. Mechanical effects suggest arrows and cannonballs firing around the theater. Lighting effects reveal the damage to the theater behind the scrim. There's even a live character who makes his way into the show—Sweetums, who goes looking for Bean Bunny.

We hope you've enjoyed this tour of Disney California Adventure as much as we have. Now you can see the Park through the eyes of an Imagineer. Look for these and so many other little gems hidden in plain sight all throughout the Park. Retrace the steps of Walt's California Adventure. But most of all, we hope you...

Enjoy the Park!

BIBLIOGRAPHY

Designing Disney: Imagineering and the Art of the Show, John Hench with Peggy Van Pelt, Disney Editions, 2003

Designing Disney's Theme Parks: The Architecture of Reassurance, Karal Ann Marling, Flammarion/CCA, 1997

Disney: The First 100 Years, Dave Smith and Steven Clark, Hyperion, 1999, rev. 2002

Disney A to Z: The Official Encyclopedia, Dave Smith, Hyperion, 1996, rev. 1998, 2006

The Disney Mountains: Imagineering at Its Peak, Jason Surrell, Disney Editions, 2007

Disneyland, Martin A. Sklar, Walt Disney Productions, 1963

Disneyland: Dreams, Traditions and Transitions, Leonard Shannon, Disney's Kingdom Editions, 1994

Disneyland: The Inside Story, Randy Bright, Harry N. Abrams, Inc., 1987

Disneyland: The Nickel Tour, David Mumford and Bruce Gordon, Camphor Tree Publishers, 1995

Disneyland Through the Decades—A Photographic Journey, Jeff Kurtti, Disney Editions, 2010

Poster Art of the Disney Parks, Danny Handke and Vanessa Hunt, Disney Editions, 2012

Remembering Walt: Favorite Memories of Walt Disney, Amy Boothe Green and Howard E. Green, Disney Editions, 1999

Walt Disney: The Triumph of the American Imagination, Neal Gabler, Alfred A. Knopf, 2006

Walt Disney, An American Original, Bob Thomas, Simon and Schuster, 1976; Hyperion, 1994

Walt Disney Imagineering: A Behind the Dreams Look at Making MORE Magic Real, The Imagineers, Disney Editions, 2010

Walt Disney Imagineering: A Behind the Dreams Look at Making the Magic Real, The Imagineers, Hyperion, 1996